GOOD NEWS Q's

By Fred Keiser
Illustrated by Dan Pegoda
Graphics by Jamison•Bell Design Associates

Grow For It Books

Published by Youth Specialties, Inc.
El Cajon, California

GOOD NEWS Q's: QUESTIONS THAT BRING THE GOSPELS TO LIFE

Grow For It Books are published by Youth Specialties, Inc., 1224 Greenfield Dr., El Cajon, California 92021.

© 1988 by Youth Specialties, Inc.

Library of Congress Cataloging-in-Publication Data
Keiser, Fred, 1947–
    Good news Q's

    (Grow for it books)
Summary: Presents guiding questions to make reading the Gospels more meaningful and their principles relevant to our present lives.

    1. Bible. N.T. Gospels—Examinations, questions, etc.—Juvenile literature. 2. Youth—Religious life. [1. Bible. N.T. Gospels—Examinations, questions, etc. 2.Christian life] I. Pegoda, Dan, ill. II. Yaconelli, Mike. III. Title. IV. Series.

BS2555.5K45 1988 226.'0076 88–277748

ISBN 0–910125–11–2

Printed in the United States of America

First printing 1988

Welcome to Good News Q's!

You are about to begin a year-long adventure through the first four books of the New Testament—Matthew, Mark, Luke, and John. These four Gospels tell the Good News of the life, death, and resurrection of Jesus. In fact, *gospel* actually means *good news*.

The Q's in *Good News Q's* are also cues—questions designed to prompt you to thoughtfully consider what the Good News is and what it means in our daily lives. Q's are thinking starters that will immediately cause you to focus on the key issue of each passage and then to discern the implications of that passage for the key issues in your life.

Q's are not test questions. They're *quest* questions—that is, they are not meant to find out how much you *know*, but rather are meant to help you grow by causing you to relate what you are reading to the decisions you make every day.

Good News Q's was written to make the Good News of Jesus become more than words on a page—and to help you translate those words into a way of life.

How To Read Good News Q's

Good News Q's has readings for 366 days. That doesn't mean you have to read every day—but if you start reading today and read one selection each day, you'll finish this book in one year (and a day).

You'll obviously need a Bible or New Testament of your own—preferably a modern translation that you like and understand. Read the passage two or three times *before* you read the questions. Think about the passage and what it means in your own life, and then begin to think about the questions referring back to the passage as often as you need. The way you study is up to you, but we do have a couple of additional suggestions that may help you even more. But don't stop with these—create your own ways of making the Good News meaningful for you.

The Biblical Reflection Method

Step 1
Quickly read through today's verses in order to get an overview of what's happening and what's being said in these verses.

Step 2
Picture in your mind the setting of today's passage. Where is the action occurring? Outside? Inside? Stormy sea or hot, arid desert? Crowded streets or quiet garden? Put the people of the passage in that setting—and put yourself somewhere in that scene, too.

Step 3
Now return to the beginning of the passage. Read each verse very slowly, acting it all out in your mind. Visualize the shimmer of the Sea of Galilee as you look at it from a distance. Hear the various voices of the disciples as they talk with Jesus. Touch the warm rock wall of the Samaritan well during the hot afternoon. Smell the meat cooking and the bread baking in the homes to which Jesus was invited to eat. Taste the dust raised by the farmer's carts and Roman chariots as you walk the several miles between towns or down a crowded street of Jerusalem during Passover. Let yourself feel what you would have felt had you been there.

Step 4
Think about your own situation at home, school, the shopping mall, at a party. In what circumstances do you

have the same sort of feelings you imagined having during the biblical scene? If you have trouble doing this, glance at the questions following today's Scripture passage. Ponder only those questions that reflect what you feel as you imagine the biblical scene.

Step 5.

Talk directly to Jesus about how you feel—about the situation he was in as well as similar situations you have had in your own life. Talk to him about any resolutions you want to make. Ask him for help with them. Thank him for his past help, and ask for strength in those areas where you need help.

Ideas/Insight Method

Step 1

Read through today's verses and try to understand the main teaching or idea.

Step 2

Think about the main idea and see if you can relate it to you and your life right now.

Step 3

Turn to the questions for today's passage and read the first one. If a question stumps you, return to the verses and read them again slowly. Then spend more time thinking about the question. *Remember—this is not a quiz or a test!* So don't get upset if you don't understand the question or how to answer it. Think about the question for as long as it's productive, and then move on to the next question.

Step 4

Now for the second question. Reread the verses that are related to the question and think about it. Continue in this pattern until you have thought through all the questions and have reread all the verses.

Step 5

Talk directly to Jesus; tell him whatever you've discovered today (in fact, you might want to keep a journal of your discoveries), whatever ideas came to you during your time of reading and reflecting. Share with him any resolutions you want to make, and ask him for his help. This might be a good time to reflect on mistakes or problem areas in your life, and then ask him for forgiveness. Or you might want to take a minute and reflect on the positive steps you are making in your life and thank him for his help as well as praise him for who he is.

Trouble-Shooter's Guide

What to do if you are having problems with your daily Bible reading.

Problem

"I just can't find time to read and study. I'm too busy to work it into my schedule."

Solution 1

Try different times. Sometimes we decide to read and study the Bible *only when we get done with everything else.* Too often that means at the very end of the day when we're too tired to do anything. So try other times:

- As soon as you get up in the morning.

- Before class or in study hall. (It's okay to put a book cover on your Bible so others won't know what it is and you won't be hassled.)

- As soon as you get home from school or work.

- Immediately before or after supper. (In the bathroom maybe? You can be by yourself, and your family will think you're just washing up.)

- Immediately before or after you do homework or a regular evening chore.

- Immediately before you go to bed.

And remember this: There is no "right" amount of time for you to read and study your Bible. Studying for five minutes is better than not studying at all. Don't get discouraged about not being able to study for an hour if you only have five minutes. Five minutes is a lot better than no minutes.

Solution 2

The Weekender Plan. Do the whole week's worth of "daily" readings on the weekend. Schedule the five Bible readings like this: The first on Friday afternoon; the second on Saturday morning; the third on Saturday night before going to sleep; the fourth at church during a quiet 5-to-10 minute slot before, during, or after the service; and the fifth on Sunday night before starting homework or before going to bed.

Problem

"Although I do my daily Bible reading, I get nothing out of it. The Bible is boring."

Solution 1

What translation of the Bible are you using? Perhaps your translation of the New Testament is too confusing for you to understand. If you frequently come across words you don't understand, you need a simpler translation. Ask your minister, priest, or youth director to help you find an easier translation.

Solution 2

How long do you give yourself for Bible reading? Remember, quantity is not as important as quality of time. Give yourself enough time to at least read the passage and questions—but if you're forcing yourself to keep studying because you think a certain amount of time is required, then you're forcing yourself to get bored. Take as long as it takes. Some days you might get done in 10 minutes. Other days you might take an hour.

Solution 3

If you are trying to do Bible study with your Walkman or Jambox blasting, it might make it difficult to concentrate. It is best to do Bible study when you are alone without any other distractions.

Solution 4

Avoid going on "automatic pilot." That happens when you come across a familiar story or portion of Scripture. It's easy to skim over familiar material, telling yourself that you already know everything there is to know from that passage. But even if you've heard a Bible story a hundred times, the Holy Spirit can still give you new ideas, new insights, or powerful feelings that you simply weren't capable of at an earlier time. When you come to a familiar part of the Gospels, get creative and see if you can find a new truth, a new idea from your study.

Solution 5

Switch methods. If you find yourself in a rut, get out of the rut by changing the way you study. Or change the location or the time you are studying. Sometimes a change in just the environment will give new life to your study.

Solution 6

Check your relationship with God. Sometimes you are unable to learn anything from God's word because your relationship with God is broken. There may be sin in your life that needs to be confessed to God. (In other words, you might knowingly be doing things you know aren't pleasing to God, but you keep hoping it won't make any difference. It will.) You may be harboring anger and bitterness towards someone and your bitterness is clouding your ability to hear God's voice.

Solution 7

Sometimes boredom and dryness are not a negative sign, but a positive sign of growth. It can mean that you are ready to go deeper in your walk with God.

We can reach a plateau in our growth at which nothing seems to be happening. We don't seem to be moving or growing. Yet this is normal. It's the calm before the storm. It's the period when our previous growth is taking root and we're getting ready to grow again. It's during times like these that we have to discipline ourselves to keep doing what got us there in the first place. We have to decide to read and study because we know that, though it's not as exciting as it used to be, the best is yet to come.

Problem

"Bible reading and prayer are supposed to help me, but they seem to disturb me more often than comfort me."

Solution 1

There is false guilt and there is legitimate guilt. False guilt is caused when you feel guilty for something you don't need to feel guilty for. For example, you may feel guilty because you aren't as good a Christian as you think you should be. It is commendable that you are not satisfied where you are in your relationship with God, but remember—*no one* is as good a Christian as they ought to be. It's good to want to improve, but guilt about it only makes it more difficult to grow.

On the other hand, there are things in our lives that need to be changed; and when we read the Bible, we often recognize the changes that need to be made. That's good. That's why we read the Bible. But once we realize that things need to be changed, it's important that we take steps to make those changes happen. Discomfort is good if it leads to a change of heart, if it leads away from sinful habits and actions, and if it brings me closer to God.

Solution 2

The discomfort you feel when you study and pray may be God's call to follow him more closely. That call always demands more effort and risk than we're used to exerting, and sometimes we just don't want to give more effort right now. But if you have what it takes to say yes to the challenge, to do what it takes to follow God more closely, then you will experience not only the hardship but the joy of following him.

Solution 3

Find a support group. You weren't intended to face the disturbing, frequently confusing challenges of the Gospel by yourself. In fact, flying solo in the Christian life can be dangerous. Find others who are praying with the Bible daily to encourage and advise you. Try to find other kids your own age to support you. You can find support from close friends, your own youth group, someone from your church, or an adult mentor that you trust. Jesus does not expect us to walk alone.

The Gospel According to

MATTHEW

▼

Ancestors aren't a big deal to most people these days. I wonder why they were so important in the Bible? How much have my parents and grandparents influenced my belief in God? Some of Jesus' ancestors were losers. I wonder why Matthew decided to mention them, anyway? Would the faith of my descendents be helped if I were listed as their ancestor?

MATT. 1:1-17

▼

Had I been Joseph, what would I have thought if my fiancèe said she was pregnant—by God? Had I been Mary, how would I have felt to know I was carrying Jesus, the Son of God (Luke 1:46-55)?

The Virgin Birth was a miracle. Do I really believe it happened? Do I believe miracles still happen today? Do I believe one could actually happen to me? Why or why not?

MATT. 1:18-25

▼

Do I have the patience of the Wise Men to wait for God? They followed a star to find Jesus—how do I find Jesus every day where I live? Herod felt threatened by Jesus—do I feel threatened by him? If so, how?

MATT. 2:1-8

▼

The Wise Men followed stars and were warned in a dream. What am I following to Jesus? How does he speak to me today? Does God even

MATT. 2:9-12

talk to me? How do I know when he is? What gifts would I give to Jesus if he were here today?

Discernment is the ability to see what people are really thinking. How did the Wise Men discern that Herod was evil and had evil intentions? When it comes to my friends, am I able to tell who's a good influence and who's a bad influence on me? When I realize that someone is a bad influence, do I have the willpower to change routes?

▼

MATT. 2:13-15

Joseph dreamed that an angel spoke to him. Do I believe that really happened? When was the last time, if ever, I felt God speaking to me? If God spoke to me through his Bible or through another person in such a way that I felt God wanted me to give up something very much a part of me—a boyfriend or girlfriend, the group of friends I hang around with, the school I now attend—would I, could I do it? Joseph at least had Mary for support. Who do I have to support me?

▼

MATT. 2:16-18

What made Herod capable of such a horrible crime? Pride? Jealousy? Insanity? Do all of us have the capability of becoming like Herod? Why or why not? Can I think of anyone living during my lifetime as evil as Herod?

When I read this passage and realize that Herod slaughtered all the male babies under two years old, does abortion cross my mind? Do I notice any similarities between what Herod did and what those who have abortions do?

▼

MATT. 2:19-23

Did I notice that what appeared at the moment like a permanent move for Joseph's family was only temporary? Did I notice that God seemed to change his mind? Do I get impatient sometimes waiting for things to change? And when I get impatient, do I sometimes become angry with God or begin doubting him?

Although Joseph did what God wanted, he was still afraid. Do I understand that even when I do the right thing, I can be afraid? Do I realize that living for God does not guarantee a life without fear or doubt?

▼

Why did the Pharisees and Sadducees—the religious leaders—have such a difficult time understanding who Jesus was? When does church get in the way of believing in Jesus?

Why did John use the word repent so much? What is repentance? Have I repented? Do I need to repent?

MATT. 3:1-17

▼

What is temptation? (See James 1:2-15.) When was the last time I was tempted? Jesus was in a weakened condition when he was tempted—he hadn't eaten anything for 40 days. When am I in a weakened condition? Jesus quoted Scripture to battle his temptation. What works for me when I am being tempted?

MATT. 4:1-11

▼

How is Jesus a light? How is Jesus a light for me? What does living in darkness mean? Have I ever lived in darkness?

Jesus said, "Repent, for the kingdom of heaven is near." Does repent mean to feel sorry for my sin, or does it mean more than that? Some people say repentance means to quit doing what I was doing. Okay, fine—but what if I do it again? Will God just keep forgiving me?

MATT. 4:12-17

▼

It's obvious that Simon Peter, Andrew, James, and John left their homes, their families, and their careers to follow Jesus. What made them do that? Could I do that? Is God calling me now to follow him? What does that mean

MATT. 4:18-22

while I'm living with my parents and going to school?

▼

MATT.
4:23-25

Jesus healed those who needed physical help. Do I believe that Jesus physically heals people today? Why or why not? Can Jesus heal other than physical things in me—things like anger, loneliness, depression, low self-esteem? Does Jesus still have the power to heal my friends, my family—even me, today?

▼

MATT.
5:1-12

The word blessed can also mean happy. Then what does happy mean? Have I experienced any of the happiness that Jesus spoke of in the eight Beatitudes (the formal name for the eight statements Jesus made here that all begin with "Blessed are..." or "Happy are...")? Why or why not?

▼

MATT.
5:13-16

Why does Jesus compare me to salt or light? What does salt do? What does light do? If I'm a Christian, do the people around me notice my saltiness, my light? How do I lose my saltiness? Does Jesus' statement "that they may see your good deeds and praise your Father in heaven" mean that I have to live a perfect life?

▼

MATT.
5:17-20

When Jesus spoke about the law, he was talking about the Ten Commandments. If Jesus came to fulfill the law, why did the Pharisees think Jesus had come to destroy it? Why does it seem that Jesus was always angering religious people? Would he threaten today's religious leaders?

▼

MATT.
5:21-26

Why is Jesus so serious about simply calling someone a fool? Can't I joke around with people a little? Is it really as important as Jesus makes it sound to interrupt whatever I'm doing in order to settle a disagreement with a friend?

▼

Why does Jesus warn me against nurturing desire for individuals merely for the sexual gratification I could get from them? How do I get rid of these desires and lusts? What does Jesus mean by "If your right hand causes you to sin, cut it off"?

MATT.
5:27-30

▼

What does Jesus think of divorce? Is he saying that divorce is justified in the case of adultery? What did Jesus mean when he said that "anyone who marries the divorced woman commits adultery"?

MATT.
5:31-32

▼

Jesus asks us to trust each other and be true to that trust so that we can speak simply, never having to swear or take an oath to support our word, even in courts. Is a society possible in

MATT.
5:33-37

which everyone can trust each other's word? If I think such a trusting society is indeed impossible, would such trust be possible within small groups? Between friends? In a family?

▼

MATT. 5:38-42

Apparently Jesus is telling us to avoid conflict, even if we are mistreated. If that's what Jesus is saying, is he correct? Can anyone live like that? What does Jesus mean when he asks me to go the extra mile? How can I go the extra mile with my friends? My family? Jesus says to not turn away from one who wants to borrow from me. What does he mean?

▼

MATT. 5:43-48

Why does Jesus ask me to love my enemies? Did he love his enemies? Do I love my enemies by allowing them to walk over me? What does Jesus mean when he instructs me to "be perfect, therefore, as your heavenly Father is perfect"?

▼

MATT. 6:1-6, 16-18

Can I help someone in need without anyone knowing about it? Isn't it normal—even right—to expect those in need to thank me for helping them? What does it mean to serve God silently?

▼

MATT. 6:7-15

Jesus said we should pray, and that "Our Father" is how we should pray. Did he mean that the Lord's Prayer is an example, or does he want us to repeat word for word the Lord's Prayer whenever we pray?

▼

MATT. 6:19-24

What is my attitude towards the things I own? Do I value them more than I do my friends? Would losing all the things I own upset me more than losing my faith and belief in God?

Is worrying a sin? Do I worry too much? Do I really believe that God will take care of my needs? All of them? If God takes care of our needs, does that mean even hunger? Does that mean he cures our cancer—or does he mean only spiritual needs? Physical needs? Emotional needs?

MATT.
6:25-34

▼

Judging means being super-critical of other people. Why is it so hard to keep from judging others? How can I stop needling or belittling others at school? How can I keep from cutting other people down? What if I examined myself first to see if I'm guilty of the same things that I criticize others for? Would it help if I tried to think of reasons behind a person's behavior before I criticize them?

MATT.
7:1-6

▼

Do I really believe these verses? Do I really expect God to help me when I ask for it? Does God give me everything I ask for? Does help come according to my plans or God's plans? How do I know what God's plan is?

MATT.
7:7-11

▼

Do I try to follow the Golden Rule in my everyday life? Have I acted this way in the past week? What occasions are there in the coming week in which I should act this way?

MATT.
7:12

▼

The Lord is saying that we can't take the easy way out and still be all that he wants us to be. Does that mean following Christ is always difficult? Does it mean that Christians are always going to be a minority? Does it mean that if I live like Christ wants me to, my friends will think I'm strange?

MATT.
7:13-14,
21-23

▼

MATT. 7:15-20	Do my friends believe the same things I do? Do they share the same morals I have? If they don't, what does that mean? Do I have only Christian friends? Should I have only Christian friends? Are my friends a positive or negative influence on me? Should one's influence on me determine whether or not to continue a friendship?

▼

MATT. 7:24-29	During the last few weeks of reading, have I pondered the words more than I usually do? Do I really believe that if I trust what God says about how to live, that my life really is built on a rock?

▼

MATT. 8:1-13	Both the leper and the Roman officer knew for certain that Jesus could help them if he wanted. Do I have that kind of faith? Does my belief or lack of belief in God change the outcome of what God does? How can I believe God more?

▼

MATT. 8:14-17, 23-34	Jesus showed his power over disease, over nature, and over Satan. Do I believe that he has that power now? That he can use it in me? Does Jesus' power work to not only heal me, but also to help me endure if I'm not healed?

▼

MATT. 8:18-22	Am I willing to follow Christ wherever he goes—or do I put conditions on following him? In verse 21 a man wasn't willing to follow Christ until the death of his father—which could have been years later. Do I do the same thing by deciding to follow Christ after I graduate from high school? After college? After marriage? After I find a job? Even now, am I saying, "I will follow you, Christ—but my friends think it's weird" or "But it might cost me my boyfriend" or "But I don't want to stop what I'm doing right now"?

Why did Jesus tell the paralytic that his sins were forgiven? Why did Jesus make such an issue of his own authority? How does it make me feel when I realize that Jesus has authority on earth to forgive sins?

    When do I feel forgiven? Is it when I've done the same sin a bunch of times? Why is it so difficult to believe that Jesus can forgive our sins—especially when we've done the same thing over and over again?

MATT.
9:1-8

▼

If Jesus didn't come to call the righteous to repentance, then it's obvious that in order to repent I have to admit I'm a sinner. That's hard. Why is it so difficult to admit that I'm a sinner? Why is it so difficult for me to admit that I need God? Is admitting that I need God a sign of weakness? Of course, if it's sinners that Jesus seeks out, then at least I'm among those he's looking for.

MATT.
9:9-13

▼

Jesus was always able to draw a crowd who'd be astonished at what he did—or who'd get extremely angry about it. Why was it usually the religious ones who were irritated by Jesus? Why is it easier to be intrigued with Jesus' miracles, or even easier to become angry with his teachings, than it is to simply follow him?

MATT.
9:14-34

▼

What does Matthew mean when he writes that Jesus had compassion on the people because they were "like sheep without a shepherd"? If to wander like sheep means to lack direction, then how does Jesus give our lives direction? Does my life have direction? Who do I know that needs direction? Is God calling me to help them?

MATT.
9:35-
10:10

▼

MATT.
10:11-
10:39

When we try to help others, we may be thanked (v. 11), rejected (v. 14), or persecuted (vv. 17ff). Do I have the strength to put up with rejection and persecution? Do I love God that much?

▼

MATT.
10:40-
11:19

How do I act towards priests and ministers of God's word? How should I act? Should they be treated differently than others?

    John was a good person who was simply trying to introduce people to Jesus—yet he was strongly criticized. Do I sometimes criticize a

genuinely good person as a goody-goody or as uncool because his goodness threatens me? What is it in me that's intimidated by one who seems to be better than me?

▼

Jesus had strong words for those who disbelieved him. Why? How can good things like education and learning get in the way of believing in God? Why does Jesus constantly imply that in order to believe in him, we have to become like children?

MATT. 11:20-30

▼

Jesus continually broke religious rules. Why? How does religion get in the way of believing in Jesus? What's good about religion? What's bad about it? What did Jesus mean when he referred to himself as Lord of the Sabbath?

MATT. 12:1-14

▼

Do I experience Jesus within me as gentle and quiet, as described by Isaiah (vv. 19,20), or do I experience him disturbing and challenging, like when he powerfully contends with the Pharisees (vv. 22-37)?

MATT. 12:15-37

▼

Why does God seem to go out of his way to make it difficult to believe in him? Why doesn't he give us clear, obvious signs? Wouldn't it be easier to believe in God if, when we asked for a miracle, we got one? Or would we be seduced by the power of miracles and forget about Jesus?

MATT. 12:38-42

▼

This is a difficult saying of Christ's. What does Jesus mean when he mentions an unoccupied house? That there are times when we're especially vulnerable to evil? When would those times be? Have I ever been especially vulnerable to sin? How do I keep that from happening?

MATT. 12:43-45

MATT. 12:46-50	Do I realize that if I do the will of the Father, then Jesus is my brother? What does a brother mean to me? What would it be like to have Jesus as my big brother?

▼

MATT. 13:1-9	What part of this parable describes me right now? What does Jesus mean by "rocky places"? What am I like if I have no root? What are the thorns in my life that surround me right now? Was the seed of faith ever really planted in my life?

▼

MATT. 13:10-23	What keeps people from understanding what Jesus is saying? What keeps me from understanding what Jesus is saying? In verse 19 Jesus says that the evil one comes along and snatches away the truth. Do I really believe in the evil one? Do I have any protection against him? (See 1 Corinthians 10:13 and Ephesians 6:10-18.)

▼

MATT. 13:24-30, 34-43	This parable implies that someday those who are evil will "get theirs." But in the meantime, what does that mean for me? How do I know whether I'm the good or the bad seed? Can anyone know?

▼

MATT. 13:31-33, 44-52	Although my faith is small, does it affect my family, my friends, my community, my world? What is the most valuable thing about my faith?

▼

MATT. 13:53-58	Have I ever felt unappreciated by my family and friends? On the other hand, have I ever taken the accomplishments or talents of my family and friends for granted? When was the last time I told someone close to me how much I loved her, or how much I admired his good qualities?

Herod was forced to do what he didn't want to do, all because of an unhealthy relationship. Are there any unhealthy relationships in my life that may influence me to do what I really don't want to do? Why is it so difficult to break off unhealthy relationships with people, even when I know they're hurting me and those around me?

MATT. 14:1-12

Do I really believe that Jesus could take five loaves and two fish and multiply the food to feed thousands? Do I really believe Jesus could take my gifts and multiply them to affect those around me? Do I believe that Jesus actually walked on water? Would I have tried walking on water like Peter? Is it okay to have doubts about Jesus?

MATT. 14:13-36

Who are the real hypocrites—those who fail to live what they believe, or those who intentionally attempt to deceive others about what they really are? Do I know any hypocrites? What does it mean to honor God with my lips, but have my heart far from him?

MATT. 15:1-9

Most of my friends swear, most of my friends lie when they have to, and most of them criticize others—all of which makes my not doing these things almost impossible. Can I actually control what comes out of my mouth by working on what enters my mind? Will reading the Bible regularly actually change how I talk and what I do? How about my thoughts? Is it harmful to merely think about doing stuff I know is wrong, as long as I don't actually do it?

Where is my mind most of the time? What am I thinking about? How do I control what I think about? Is it even possible to control my thoughts? Someone has said that you can't stop random thoughts from popping

MATT. 15:10-20

into your head—but you can decide whether to keep them there. Do I agree?

▼

MATT. 15:21-28

When I have a genuine need, am I willing to keep asking Jesus for help until he helps me? The woman argued with God. Am I afraid to argue with God?

▼

MATT. 15:29-31

Do I ever have the faith to ask God for help and healing? Do I really expect anything extraordinary to happen because of my prayers? Does Jesus have the same power now as he did 2,000 years ago?

▼

MATT. 15:32-39

Jesus had fed a few thousand other people another time under almost the same circumstances. Although his disciples observed the miracle on the previous occasion, this time they still wondered how Jesus would feed the crowd. Am I like the disciples—forgetting the Lord's power even when I fall into the identical problem he helped me with before?

▼

MATT. 16:1-4

Are there people in my life (friends, teachers, co-workers, other adults) who ask me to prove my faith through signs or evidence? Am I aware of the "signs of the times" in my own life? Do I see the hand of God directing me through others?

The "sign of Jonah" refers not only to Jonah's preaching to the people of Ninevah without performing any miracles, but also to the three days he spent in the whale. (See the Old Testament book of Jonah.) The new sign of Jonah is the resurrection of Jesus from the dead after three days in the tomb. Do I believe in the resurrection?

▼

Is it encouraging to realize that the disciples often misunderstood Jesus? It's easy to romanticize the disciples as a group of strong, authoritative men who never wavered in their faith and always understood exactly what Jesus was saying.

MATT. 16:5-12

     The truth is, they were a dissimilar bunch of men who fought among themselves and were usually too dense to understand who Jesus was, not to mention what he was talking about. They were forceful and zealous one day, and then frightened the next. In short, they were just like me. How did Jesus respond to their humanness? Does Jesus understand me?

▼

Who do I say that Jesus is?

MATT. 16:13-20

MATT. 16:21- 28	What does it mean to deny myself? Do I assume that if I want something, then it probably isn't what God wants for me? What does it mean to "take up my cross"? Is following Christ difficult for everyone or just for those who aren't very good Christians? What did Jesus mean when he said, "Whoever loses his life for me will find it"?

▼

MATT. 17:1-8, 14-21	Have I ever felt so close to God that I could touch him? Why doesn't God let us feel that way all the time? If I had an intimate experience with God like Peter did, would I want to hang on to the experience, just like Peter? Why? Though the disciples had just experienced God in a powerful way, they could not heal a little boy. Why? Do I really believe verse 20? Can anyone ever have that much faith?

▼

MATT. 17:9-13	Has God sent prophets into my life who, like Elijah, pointed out things I was doing wrong and challenged me to change my behavior? Did I accept these "Elijahs" as people who told me God's will, or did I reject them and their advice?

▼

MATT. 17:22- 27; 22:15- 22	Why was Jesus exempt from paying taxes? Why did he pay them, anyway? What light does Matthew 22:15-22 shed on this subject? When do I obey the government (Caesar), and when do I say no to it? Do I have the courage to say no to the government if I know it will cost me?

▼

MATT. 18:1-9; 19:13- 15	Why do we need to be like little children? What are some childlike qualities I need? Jesus sounds like he takes sin seriously. Do I? Am I willing to get rid of sin in my life, or do I keep

hanging on to it, thinking it will go away on its own? What does Jesus mean when he says, "If your hand or foot causes you to sin, cut it off"?

▼

Does Jesus really mean that each of us has a guardian angel? Does God actually try to protect our innocence? How do we lose our innocence?

MATT. 18:10-11

▼

Do I realize that God loves me enough that, instead of waiting for me to track him down, he seeks me? What causes me to wander away from him? What does it mean to be lost? Do I allow myself to be found, or do I avoid God's love? When I sin, do I immediately seek God or do I run even further away from him? Why do I even try hiding from God after I sin?

MATT. 18:12-14

▼

Why is it difficult to confront a friend when they've done something wrong? Am I willing to confront brothers or sisters when they've blown it? Jesus said that if the person I confront doesn't listen, I'm to take one or two others with me and confront the person again. Under what circumstances, if any, would I be willing to do that?

If my friend still refuses, Jesus says to take the problem to the church. What does that mean? Do I respect the authority of the church to discipline those whose behavior is a problem?

MATT. 18:15-20

▼

When I've been wronged, it's hard to forgive someone once, let alone seven times. Have I forgiven anyone even twice? What prevents me from forgiving people? Will I be forgiven by God if I don't forgive others? Does the fact that I cannot forgive others influence my relationship with God at all? What can possibly give me strength to forgive the unforgivable?

MATT. 18:21-35

MATT. 19:1-12

It's not easy to stay married these days. What will I do in my dating relationships to avoid divorce when I get married? Is divorce a sin? Does God forgive those who are divorced? Jesus implies that, since keeping a marriage commitment is difficult, marriage isn't for everyone (v. 11). Is it for me?

▼

MATT. 19:16-30

Do I have the kind of trust in God my Father so that I am willing to sacrifice my material possessions in order to do his will and know that he'll take care of me? Am I so concerned about the things of life—the objects of my possession—that I have no time left for God? Why does a swelling bank account increase the difficulty of serving Christ? Do I honestly believe that if I forget about material possessions and simply serve God, I will receive a hundred times as much in spiritual blessings? If I believe this, how can I live it out each day?

▼

MATT. 20:1-16

Isn't it unfair for a person who worked one hour to be paid as much as the person who worked eight hours? What do I think Jesus meant in verses 13-14 when he said, "Friend, I am not being unfair to you...Don't I have the right to do what I want with my own money?"

I know God is incredibly generous with me—so why should it bother me that God is incredibly generous with others? What did Jesus mean when he warned that "the last will be first, and the first will be last"? Am I willing to let go of my rights for the sake of others?

▼

MATT. 20:17-28

"People must have the second-to-the-last word before the last word," wrote a theologian. He meant that often we want the prize without having to work for it.   Some disciples wanted to sit at Jesus' right hand. Jesus asked them if they were willing to endure what he was about to endure—death by crucifixion. Filled with more enthusiasm than wisdom, they answered yes.

Am I willing to suffer for following Jesus? Am I willing to risk losing my friends because of Jesus? Am I willing to risk my boyfriend or girlfriend because of Jesus? Am I more concerned about what Christ wants me to do right now? What does it mean to be a slave of Jesus?

▼

Am I a compassionate person? Do I show mercy to those less fortunate than myself? Do I reach out to those who are handicapped?

MATT. 20:29-34

▼

If Jesus showed up at my school, would I cheer for him in front of my friends?

Do I realize that the same people who welcomed Jesus into the city only a few days later shouted, "Crucify him!"? Why were the crowds so fickle? Am I that way? Do I cheer Christ when things are going my way, and then get mad at him when my life changes direction?

MATT. 21:1-11

▼

Jesus was outraged at the misuse of God's temple. What in our society causes me to be outraged? If it was okay for Jesus to get angry, under what conditions is it okay for me? What Jesus did took a lot of courage. Do I have courage? How do I get courage? Do I care about the injustice I see around me enough to do anything about it? Do I believe that even today there are still people who appreciate when the right thing is done even if it's the more difficult, less popular thing to do?

MATT. 21:12-17

▼

Jesus acted symbolically: he cursed the fig tree to show that religion had withered and produced no fruit. Have I let my religion

MATT. 21:18-27

become so routine that it's as fruitless and dried up as the religion in Jesus' time? Sure, the chief priests and elders asked a lot of questions—but they really didn't want to hear Jesus' answers. Do I really want to know what Jesus thinks about questions I have inside? Do I sometimes hide behind my questions because I really don't want to hear his answers?

▼

MATT. 21:28-32

Which person am I—the one who rebels and complains about God's call and God's commands, but who eventually follows them? Or the one who gets excited enough to say yes to God's command—but when it comes down to actually doing something, doesn't do anything? Have I had a sincere change of heart like the tax collectors and prostitutes Jesus speaks about, so that now I sincerely try to follow God's will?

We have so much freedom to worship in this country that it's easy to be a Christian. Do I take my freedom for granted and, as a result, not take my faith seriously? Am I in danger of squandering my opportunity for faith because it seems so easy and accessible?

MATT. 21:33-46

▼

Is it possible that those who've lacked opportunity to hear about Christ, yet who sincerely seek God's will, could be closer to God than me? What did Jesus mean when he said that "many are invited, but few are chosen"?

MATT. 22:1-14

▼

(See Matthew 17:22-27.)

MATT. 22:15-22

▼

Do I actually believe in heaven? What will heaven be like? Does it sound inviting to me? What difference does it make if I believe in heaven and hell?

MATT. 22:23-33

▼

Do I try to live by the two greatest commandments? Every time the Pharisees tried to trap or trick Jesus with their questions, Jesus came up with an answer that both answered their questions and silenced them. When I have questions or problems with life and with God, do I bring my questions and problems to Jesus in prayer and give him quiet time to answer them?

MATT. 22:34-46

▼

Do I try to impress my friends and family with how godly I am, or do I simply try to please God? Is my desire to be accepted and well thought of by my peers stronger than my desire to be well thought of by God?

MATT. 23:1-12

▼

MATT. 23:13-28

Why was Jesus so harsh with the Pharisees? Am I guilty of the kind of hypocrisy that the Pharisees were? Do I pretend to be religious around my youth group, the church, my pastor or priest—but then act totally different when I'm around my friends? Do I practice Christianity on Sunday or at church activities, but then ignore it during the week?

▼

MATT. 23:29-39

Jesus pointed out that Israel's religious leaders had persecuted God's prophets throughout the nation's history. In other words, being true to God's law and being popular are often mutually exclusive.

Have I been persecuted or rejected for standing up for my religious beliefs, morals, and practices? If I haven't, is it because I'm lucky enough to have Christian friends and family, or because I really don't live or talk about my faith openly before others— especially before those who don't live Christian lives?

▼

MATT. 24:1-14

Here and in the sections that follow, Jesus talks about two things: the destruction of Jerusalem, which occurred 40 years after he predicted it and 10 to 15 years after Matthew wrote this gospel; and about the last judgment and the end of the world.

Both of these events—Jerusalem's destruction and the end of the world—remind us that nothing on earth is permanent and reassure us that Jesus' kingdom is not an earthly kingdom. How can this change the way I live my day? Do I sometimes live as though this life is all there is? Am I able to let go of the things of this life?

▼

MATT. 24:15-31

Do I really believe there are false prophets and false Christs in the world? I've heard of mentally unbalanced people who think they are Christ. But are there any people living today who think they are saviors of the world—and their followers actually believe that they are? What about Khomeini and Qaddafi?

Jesus is saying, of course, that one day he'll return. Yet that's not all. He's also saying that the days preceding his return will be pretty awful. Should I spend my energy wondering exactly when Jesus will return, or should I live my life as though he might return any minute? That's a loaded question—but if I thought Jesus was coming back today, what difference would it make in the way I live?

▼

What did Jesus mean when he told us to "keep watch" for his return?

MATT. 24:32-51

▼

Who do I most resemble—the five wise, prepared women or the five foolish, unprepared women? How do I prepare myself not only for the future, but for the struggles of each day? Have I prepared myself by cultivating good habits that will strengthen me against temptation and weakness? Have I put time and energy into getting to know God and his will in everyday things so that I'll be able to recognize his voice and his will as problems arise later in life?

MATT. 25:1-13

▼

Am I aware of the talents Jesus has given me? Do I believe I have any worthwhile talents? Have I buried my faith and talents within myself and kept quiet for fear of being put down or criticized? How can I invest my talents and gifts?

MATT. 25:14-30

▼

Do I really believe that when I help someone who is hungry or poor, I am helping Jesus? Do I consciously invest my time and energy in the elderly, the handicapped, the poor, the hurting? Do I realize just how much I can do?

MATT. 25:31-46

MATT. 26:1-16

Jesus knew suffering and death were coming to him—yet he didn't sidestep them. When I see suffering coming my way, do I try to avoid it? Should I try to avoid suffering? Do I believe that suffering and persecution for Christ is a part of every true Christian's life, just as it was of Jesus' life?

▼

MATT. 26:17-30

When Jesus suggested that someone at the table would betray him, each of the disciples thought it was him. Why? Do I sometimes feel like I've betrayed Christ? What was Jesus saying to the disciples when he took bread and said, "This is my body"? When he took the wine and said, "This is my blood of the covenant"? Do I appreciate and take advantage of communion?

▼

MATT. 26:31-35

Peter thought he didn't have it in him to deny Christ. Have I ever been in situations where I thought I was strong enough to handle temptations, but it turned out I wasn't strong enough? (At a party where there was drinking, for example, and I thought I could keep from drinking; or with a boyfriend or girlfriend with whom I thought I could resist sexual temptation.) What can I do to remind myself of my vulnerability? Am I also aware that, though Peter did what Jesus predicted, Jesus still loved him and forgave him?

▼

MATT. 26:36-46

Do I realize that Jesus experienced genuine fear and anxiety as his suffering and death approached? Does that help me when I experience fear and anxiety? When I am fearful or anxious, do I take those fears and anxieties directly to God like Jesus did? When I'm faced with a difficult decision, do I really believe that the Father will give me the strength I need to do what's right?

The disciples could not stay awake with

Jesus though they knew he was suffering and hurting. What did Jesus mean by his statement, "The spirit is willing, but the body is weak"? Do I experience that frustration in my own life? What can be done about it?

▼

The only way the apostles knew how to react to betrayal and violence was with violence. When Jesus asked them to respond with peace, meekness, and strength, they fled. Is revenge, anger, and hostility the way I usually react when people hurt me or threaten me? Am I brave enough to respond with love and peace and meekness to those who hurt me? How do I get to a place where I can forgive those who hurt me?

MATT. 26:47-56

▼

Jesus was innocent of the false charges and knew it. He also knew that to admit that he was the Messiah would mean death. He told the truth.

MATT. 26:57-68

When we believe something to be true, is it easier to admit it—even if it may cost us? In other words, does truth give us courage? Would I have been able to tell the truth in the situation Jesus was in? Do I have any idea how much patience and inner strength Jesus had to be able to resist the taunts and ridicule of his accusers?

▼

MATT. 26:69-75

In what ways do I deny Jesus each day? Peter recognized immediately that he had denied Christ, felt remorse and guilt, then began to change. Do I, too, recognize my denials and feel sorry for them? Am I taking steps to avoid denying Christ again like I have in the past?

▼

MATT. 27:1-10

For whatever reasons, Judas' betrayal of Jesus didn't turn out as he anticipated: overwhelmed by despair, he took his own life. I too often assume that I can always turn away from my sin, I can always repent and come back to God. Has it occurred to me that sin has consequences—and that those consequences aren't always what I thought they were? Does it occur to me that sin can sometimes blind my thinking and make it impossible for me to come back to God?

▼

MATT. 27:11-26

Pilate clearly knew what was right. Though he wanted to release Jesus, he was rolled over by the pressure and threats of the crowd, finally trying to convince himself and others that it wasn't his responsibility, anyway.

Has that ever happened to me? Have I ever wanted to do right and tried to convince others to go along with me, but I eventually yielded to their pressure? Do I try to pass off the responsibility for my actions to someone else? Do I too easily blame my parents, my friends, my school for my own actions?

When I read this account of the crucifixion of Christ, do I realize just how much suffering Jesus endured for me? Do I realize that Jesus could have saved himself, could have freed himself from the cross? Have I ever pondered the consequences if Jesus had taken that option?

MATT. 27:27-44

Jesus recited the first line of Psalm 22, a psalm that predicted the sufferings Jesus was experiencing at that moment. Roman guards made an astonishing statement: "Surely he was the Son of God!" Do I believe that Jesus truly was the Son of God? Do I believe this enough to make Jesus and his teachings and his values the most important thing in my life?

MATT. 27:45-56

Was I aware of the extreme lengths that the Jewish leaders and the Roman government went to in order to prevent Jesus' followers from stealing his body and faking a resurrection? Do I see similar extremes today in the way society tries to discredit Jesus and belief in God? Do I realize that many people today look upon Jesus as a liar and imposter just as in Jesus' time? What can I do in my own life each day to communicate to people that Jesus is still alive and well?

MATT. 27:57-66

The soldiers were eyewitnesses to the resurrection of Christ, yet they agreed to spread the lie that Jesus' body was stolen. Have I knowingly gone along with what I knew to be false because I didn't want to be ridiculed or rejected? The evidence for the resurrection may not be entirely admissible in a court of law—but even if we did have absolute physical proof, would it cause more people to believe in Jesus?

Why or why not? How do I know that the resurrection is true?

MATT. 28:1-15

MATT. 28:16-20	Why do I think that theologians call this "The Great Commission"? What is Jesus calling all disciples to do? Does his call include me? Do I really believe that Jesus and his power and help are truly present with me now and will be present with me forever?

The Gospel According to

MARK

▼

Do I realize that almost every detail about the coming of Jesus was predicted in the Old Testament? John the Baptist came to announce the coming of Jesus. Do I, in effect, have the same role today? How do I let my friends know that Jesus was the Messiah?

MARK 1:1-11

▼

Why did the Holy Spirit send Jesus to the desert for 40 days? Do I ever feel the need to be alone with God for an extended period of time? Why don't I spend more time alone with God? Have I ever felt the Holy Spirit confirm in my heart that God is pleased to love me and be my Savior? Have I ever asked God to let me know that he's pleased with me?

MARK 1:12-13

▼

Simon Peter, Andrew, James, and John left everything behind to follow Jesus. Am I willing to leave behind friends, family, and school in order to follow God's plan for me? Am I willing to spend more time doing that which will lead me closer to God?

MARK 1:14-20

▼

Do I believe that there are evil spirits? Do I believe that evil is something to be taken seriously? The demons said they knew who Jesus was (vv. 23-24, 34), yet he didn't want them to tell the people (vv. 25, 34). Why?

MARK 1:21-28,34

▼

MARK
1:29-39

Do I really believe Jesus can heal people? The Bible says that Jesus "went off to a solitary place, where he prayed." Do I do that? Daily? Weekly? Regularly? Why did Jesus avoid the crowds?

▼

MARK
1:40-45

Jesus did not want people to come to him just because of his healing power. Why do I follow Christ? Because of what he can do for me, or for what I can do for him?

▼

MARK
2:1-12

Friendships are difficult to find today. The friends of the paralytic were willing to go to extremes to help him. Am I willing to go to extremes for my friends? Jesus healed the paralytic and, in the process, upset many religious people. How can my religion get in the way of following Jesus?

▼

MARK
2:13-17

Jesus asked a tax collector who was very rich and powerful—and apparently very unhappy—to follow him. Do I take time with my friends to realize that what's on the outside may not represent what's going on inside of them? Matthew was obviously ready to follow Jesus. How many of my friends are ready—but because I haven't checked them out, I don't know it?

What do these verses tell me about the kinds of people I hang around with? If I hang around non-Christians, then I have to be that much more careful that they don't influence me negatively. How do I determine when the people I hang out with are encouraging my relationship with God or blocking it?

▼

MARK
2:18-22

Fasting isn't practiced often in our society. Fasting is simply not eating for a period of time in order to concentrate on my relationship with God. Why don't I try to fast for one day and see if thinking only about God for a day makes a difference in the way I live?

▼

Jesus openly challenged religious rules and regulations that had nothing to do with following him. He consequently angered the religious leaders enough that they wanted to kill him. Do I have the courage to say no to religious rules and regulations that I know have nothing to do with following Jesus (e.g., hair length, facial hair, musical styles)?

MARK 2:23-3:6

▼

The crowds came to Jesus because he did miracles, yet Jesus prohibited even the evil spirits from telling who he was. Could it be that Jesus was concerned that people would follow him for the wrong reasons? What are some wrong reasons for following Christ? Why am I following him?

MARK 3:7-12

▼

Like the disciples, do I feel that I have a special calling from God to follow him? What has God appointed me to do specifically where I am right now?

MARK 3:13-19

▼

Some thought that Jesus' power came from evil forces. Have I ever heard of anyone who had great powers, but I thought they were evil? How can I distinguish between the power of evil and the power of good in my life?

MARK 3:20-30

▼

What does it mean to be a brother or sister to Jesus? What kind of a brother or sister am I to Jesus? How could I do a better job of being a brother or sister?

MARK 3:31-35

▼

MARK 4:1-20

This isn't really a parable of a sower, but of soils. What kind of soil am I? Has the seed of genuine faith ever been planted in me? If it has, how can I improve the soil? How can I identify the thorns in my life? How can I combat the "worries of this life, the deceitfulness of wealth, and the desires for other things"?

▼

MARK 4:21-25

Am I willing to let my thoughts and actions out in the open? Do I realize that the closer I am to God, the more willing I am to be honest about who I really am? Even though nothing is hidden from God, do I nonetheless try to hide things from him? Although I have weaknesses that would embarrass me if others knew about them, do I still judge others when I see their weaknesses?

▼

MARK 4:26-34

Could these two parables help me when I become discouraged about the snail's pace of my spiritual growth and the little change I see in me? Do I realize that God is working within me even when I don't notice it, that it's often noticed by others before it is by me? Do I realize that growth doesn't mean that I become spiritually mature overnight? Do I understand that since I'm always growing, it's difficult to notice? So how can I know when I'm growing, anyway?

▼

MARK 4:35-41

While the storm raged, Jesus slept. Have I ever had stormy occasions in my life when I thought God was asleep? Have I ever felt like the disciples when they asked Jesus, "Don't you care if we drown?" Have I ever really been afraid? If I have been afraid, did I trust God to watch over my spiritual welfare? How much faith do I have in God?

▼

When Jesus cured the demoniac (the man so possessed and dangerous, he had to be chained), the people asked Jesus to leave. Why, especially after the good that he did for the man? Would I have asked Jesus to leave?

MARK 5:1-14

Sometimes we really don't want a bad situation changed because we're threatened by something new and different. Have I ever wanted things to change but been afraid that the changes would inconvenience me too much? Am I willing to be inconvenienced by Jesus if I know things will be better between him and me?

▼

After the man had been healed, Jesus told him to return home and tell his family and neighbors what God had done for him. Instead, the man wanted to follow Jesus. It's much harder to tell my family and friends about Jesus than to travel and talk to strangers. Why is that?

MARK 5:15-20

Is God asking me to talk to my neighbors and family first before tackling a less personal task for God?

▼

MARK 5:21-24a,35-42

Jairus and his friends limited God's power, for they thought he could heal the sick but not raise the dead. Do I limit God's power toward me?

▼

MARK 5:15-20,43

In contrast to what he told the man exorcised of demons (vv. 15-20), Jesus told Jairus and his wife to tell no one about the miracle of their daughter's healing (v. 43). Why did God act one way with the healed demoniac, and another way with Jairus? Does God ask me to do things that are different from what he asks someone else to do?

▼

MARK 5:24b-34

In the middle of a pushing and shoving crowd, Jesus felt the touch of a hurting woman. Do I believe that Jesus has time for me when I hurt? Do I believe it enough to reach out to God for healing?

▼

MARK 6:1-6

Why is it easier to respect strangers than those we know and are familiar with? Do I take my family and friends for granted? How could I show them that I really do respect and admire them?

▼

MARK 6:7-13

Jesus sent the apostles out with no money or resources, expecting them to be provided for by those that they preached to. Do I think that is still valid today? Should ministers and priests depend on those they preach to?

▼

Herod liked to hear what John the Baptist said, even though the prophet disturbed him by challenging him to change his life. But in the end Herod went along with his peers and his lusts and had John the Baptist executed.

MARK 6:14-29

When I read the Bible, do I find the words there hard to listen to because they require me to change? Is it easier to listen to my friends and my lusts than to the words of God?

▼

Jesus assumed responsibility for his hungry listeners. His disciples, on the other hand, didn't like the idea of feeding a few thousand people. Who am I usually like when I see people in need—Jesus or his disciples?

MARK 6:30-56

▼

Jesus said that Isaiah was right when he prophesied that "people honor me with their lips, but their hearts are far from me." What does that mean? Have I ever felt like that? What exactly is my "heart"? How do I keep it close to God?

MARK 7:1-23

▼

After all the things Christ did, the Pharisees still asked for an instant miracle as proof of Christ's claims. Do I ever test God by asking for a sign? Do I ever ask God for proof of his love for me?

MARK 7:24- 8:13

▼

First Jesus points out that the apostles just don't see, just don't understand his words (v. 18)—and then we read of the gradual healing of a man's blindness (vv. 22-25). Am I still blind to the meaning of Christ in my life? The Apostle Paul says that "the god of this age has blinded the minds of unbelievers" (2 Corinthians 4:4). What does he mean? Have I ever been blinded by the "god of this age"? How do I regain my sight?

MARK 8:14-26

MARK
8:27-38

Peter declared that, yes, Jesus was the Messiah—and then immediately exposed his ignorance of what Jesus meant and of the demands on himself because Jesus was the Messiah. Do I know what it means for Jesus to be the Messiah? Do I understand what it means in my everyday life if Jesus is the Messiah? Have I carefully counted the cost of following Christ?

▼

MARK
9:1-13

The disciples had an exhilarating mountaintop experience—yet with no idea of its significance. While they wanted to stay on the mountain, Jesus was telling them that he had suffering to look forward to. We'd all rather stay on the mountain than suffer.

Do I understand the role of suffering in the Christian life? Do I understand that inspiring experiences are not for holding on to indefinitely, but are memories that can keep me going during the rough times? What mountaintop experiences do I remember in my life?

▼

MARK
9:14-29

Jesus could do things the apostles could not do. Why? The disciples asked the same question in verse 28 and Jesus' response was, "This kind can come out only by prayer." What did Jesus mean? In verse 23 Jesus says that "everything is possible for him who believes." Do I believe that? Why or why not?

▼

MARK
9:30-41

The humanity of the disciples is obvious in these verses. Because they were so caught up with the prestige of being associated with Jesus, they were blind to human suffering and unable to hear what Jesus was saying.

Have I ever fallen into that trap? Have I ever been so concerned about my status at school and with my friends that I am unable to hear Jesus or to see suffering? How do I get my focus back on Christ?

Jesus stressed the seriousness of leading others away from God. Have I ever led others away from God? Am I doing that now? How do I stop leading them away from and start pointing them towards God?

MARK 9:42-50

▼

Jesus is clear about what he thinks of divorce: although it is allowed in certain cases (what are those cases?), it is not what God intends. How do I feel about divorce? Do I believe it is even possible in this day and age to get married and stay married? If Jesus were here, what would he say about living together without marriage?

MARK 10:1-12

▼

After Jesus stressed the necessity of becoming like a child, a rich man could not follow him because he would not let go of his possessions. What is my attitude towards my possessions? Am I willing to part with them? Am I willing to share them? What does it mean to give my possessions to God?

MARK 10:13-27

▼

Do I really believe that if I follow Christ—even if it means giving up a lot—that it will be worth it? Be careful—to be a follower of Christ does not mean everything will be wonderful. My faith will cost me a lot. What will it cost me? Am I willing to pay that cost to follow Jesus? Jesus told his disciples that he would die and then rise again. Why? How does the death and resurrection of Jesus affect me and my commitment to Jesus?

MARK 10:28-34

▼

James and John were a lot like us—they wanted all the benefits of knowing Christ without having to work for it. How do I do that? Do I ever want forgiveness without repentance? Do I ever want God to get me out of a jam without dealing with how I got in the jam in the first

MARK 10:35-45

place? Do I ever want all the good things (happiness, joy, fulfillment, peace) without any of the hard things (prayer, Bible reading, waiting, suffering, struggling, working)?

Do Christians feel like they're better than non-Christians? Do I make my non-Christian friends feel like they're not as "together" as me? How?

▼

MARK 10:46-52

Read 2 Corinthians 4:1-6. In what ways am I blinded? Do I ask God to help me when I feel blinded, unable to see what God is doing in me? Jesus said that the faith of Bartimaeus healed him. What did Jesus mean by that? How can my faith heal my blindness?

▼

MARK 11:1-10

The disciples did what Jesus asked even when they had no clue about what he meant. Am I willing to do what Christ tells me in his Word even when I see no reasons for obeying, no results from obeying?

48

It was easy to follow Christ on Palm Sunday, but much harder to follow and be loyal to him on Good Friday. Do I follow Christ only when it's easy, or am I willing to follow him even when it's difficult?

▼

With one long look at the temple, Jesus knew that it was no longer a means by which people could reach God. His cursing of the fig tree the next day was a prophetic and symbolic way for him to show that the Temple of the Old Testament Jewish religion was itself no longer suitable to lead us to God.

When I find that friends, songs, movies, videos, or other influences are no longer a means for me to find and reach God, do I have the courage of Jesus to denounce those things and oppose their use for myself and others? How can I develop the kind of courage that Jesus had when he threw the merchants out of the temple? How can I develop the wisdom needed to know when something in my life no longer brings me closer to God?

MARK 11:11-21

▼

First of all, do I have enough faith even to ask God for something? Second, do I think there are certain things I cannot ask God for? Third, what does it mean for someone to believe but to yet "doubt in his heart"? Furthermore, it sounds like my prayers will be affected if I remain angry with someone. Why does Christ say that? How can my anger towards someone affect not only my prayers, but the rest of my life as well? How can I get the strength to forgive someone who has wronged me?

MARK 11:22-26

▼

Nothing was wrong with the questions the Pharisees asked Jesus—what was wrong was their motives for asking the questions. For they didn't want an answer: they just wanted to catch him up.

MARK 11:27-33

I have a lot of questions for Jesus, too. Nothing's wrong with those questions—unless they're based on my frustration with his answers or his silence. Am I upset with Jesus because he doesn't seem to be responding the way I want him to? Do I ever question God because his teaching is too difficult or inconvenient, or because the Bible forbids me doing things I want to do? Does reading the Bible, even if it doesn't give me all the answers I need, at least help me to know if my questions have the right motives? How?

▼

MARK 12:1-12

The owner of the vineyard kept sending servants, and the servants kept getting beaten and killed. Who are the servants that God keeps sending to me? Parents? Teachers? Church workers, pastors, priests, and youth workers? Friends? In what ways do I reject them? How should I respond to them? The tenants rejected even the vineyard owner's own son. Is there any reason why I might reject Jesus himself if he came to me personally? What areas am I reluctant to let Jesus oversee? Boyfriend, girlfriend, drinking, partying, sex? The vineyard's tenants were obviously angry and threatened. Am I very defensive about anything? Slow to listen to anyone about changing my behavior? What can I do about that?

▼

MARK 12:13-17

The people in this confrontation with Jesus were, in Mark's word, "amazed" at the courage and wisdom of Jesus. What is courage? Am I as courageous in answering my friends' criticisms of my faith as Jesus was in this confrontation with Pharisees? Where does courage come from? How do I get it? Where in my life do I need more courage?

▼

Was this a sincere question by the Sadducees, or were they using this question to merely avoid dealing with who Christ was? Do I use questions as excuses to avoid doing what I know I should do?

MARK 12:18-27

▼

This is the fifth consecutive confrontation between Jewish authorities and Jesus since he disrupted the selling and money-changing in the Temple (11:15-17). Do I realize that some problems in my life never go away? Do I realize that some things in life will always be there? That I will have to struggle with them forever? Where can I find the strength to combat problems I have to live with? What does it mean to be "not far from the kingdom of God"? Do I have any friends like this? How can I help them get closer?

MARK 12:28-34

▼

Religion can apparently not only get in the way of genuine faith, but actually keep us from faith altogether. What's dangerous about religion? What religious things that I do keep me from having a relationship with Jesus? Do I know any people in my life who are religious but don't know God? Should I confront them like Jesus did or quietly hope they see their error?

MARK 12:35-44

▼

Sooner or later everyone endures times when their faith is severely challenged or tested. It may be the death of a friend or family member, a serious illness or accident, a period of severe depression, rejection by a boyfriend or girlfriend, divorce, physical or sexual abuse, etc. Have I ever had those times? Will I have more times like that? Even though this particular passage is talking about the future persecution of the church, what does Jesus say in this passage that could help me when I am tested (vv. 9,11,13)?

MARK 13:1-13

MARK 13:14-27

Do I really believe in the bodily return of Jesus to earth (what some call the Second Coming)? Do I believe that the end of the world will come soon, many centuries from now, or never? What does it mean to "be on your guard"? If Jesus came today, would I be glad or sad? Why?

▼

MARK 13:28-37

Whether I meet Christ at the end of the world, at the Second Coming, or through my own death, how can I keep myself ready to meet him?

▼

MARK 14:1-11

Am I like the woman who defied the logic and opinions of the powerful, responding instead out of her love for Jesus—or am I more likely to deny my love for Christ and his love for me, and thereby betray him? Why is it always so easy, so tempting to side with those who are against Jesus? Who are those people in my life?

▼

MARK 14:12-21

How does it feel when I cannot trust a friend? How did Jesus feel, knowing that his own disciple, his own friend, was about to betray him? Have I ever been betrayed by a friend? How did I respond afterwards? Did I forgive that person? Can I forgive now?

▼

MARK 14:22-26

How important is communion (or Eucharist)? Why has the Church continued this ritual for all these centuries? Have I ever had a communion or Eucharistic experience where I truly felt the presence of God? What happens to the bread, to the wine, to me during communion?

▼

MARK 14:27-31

Like Peter and the other disciples, am I a fair-weather friend, comfortable and confident with my Christian faith as long as it is not seriously challenged? Am I super-confident about my faith, or do I wonder if something might happen to cause me to quit believing? Is there anything I can think of that would cause me to quit believing in Christ? The older we get, it seems, the more difficult it is to believe. Why is that? What can I do now to ensure that I won't quit believing when I get older?

▼

Can Jesus better understand and forgive my weaknesses because he himself was tempted to similar weaknesses—by not wanting to die, for example, even though he knew his father wanted him to? (Read Hebrews 2:14-18; 4:14-16.)

MARK 14:32-36

▼

Was I aware that even the apostles had difficulty praying, difficulty staying awake during their prayers, difficulty avoiding distractions, difficulty sticking with prayer?

MARK 14:37-42

Does that encourage me in my own struggles with prayer?

▼

MARK 14:43-52

Jesus was deserted by everyone. If I had been there, would I have deserted him then? Have there been times in my life when I have deserted him? Will I ever get to the point in my life where I'm certain I won't desert him?

▼

MARK 14:53-65

Jesus remained silent before his accusers. Do I realize how powerful silence can be? How can I learn to be silent more often?

▼

MARK 14:66-72

What are the differences, if any, between Judas's betrayal and Peter's betrayal? They responded differently to their betrayals of Jesus. What were the differences? How should I respond to my betrayals of Christ?

▼

MARK 15:1-15

Who was responsible for Jesus' death? It would have been easy for Pilate to blame the people who were screaming for Jesus to be crucified—but it wasn't that easy. How many times do I hide behind the mistakes of others to cover my own wrongs? Do I find it difficult to take responsibility for my own decisions, or do I constantly try to find someone else to blame? What can I do to start assuming responsibility for my decisions?

▼

MARK 15:16-20

What do I think would have been more difficult for Jesus—the pain or the humiliation? How could Jesus just stand there while people spit on him and mocked him, when all he had to do was flex his power and reduce his enemies to dust? Have I ever been humiliated in front of others? Can I imagine how Jesus must have felt? What do I think gave Jesus the power to keep silent? Is that power available to me?

Jesus was treated like a common criminal, yet was guilty of no crime. Does that comfort me when I am falsely accused or put in an unfair category (nerd, religious fanatic, etc.)? This sounds almost silly compared to what Jesus went through—but when I am grounded, even if it's unjust (though isn't it usually because I deserve it?), can I accept it with peace and love as Jesus did? Should I accept injustice with peace and love?

MARK 15:21-32

▼

While enduring the agonies of death, Jesus prayed an Old Testament psalm that begins as a prayer of complaint, but soon turns around and reaffirms faith in God. Am I able to pray my complaints to God as well as my requests? Can I actually work out some of my unhappiness even as I'm praying to God? Like the soldier, do I think that the manner of Jesus' death proves that he really is the Son of God? Do I grasp the fact that Jesus' death on the cross was for me? Does that truth have an impact on my daily life?

MARK 15:33-41

▼

Joseph of Arimathea displayed much courage by willingly admitting his association with Christ after the crucifixion. Would I have had that kind of courage? Was I aware that Pilate took extra precautions to make sure that Jesus was actually dead? Does this fact strengthen my belief and faith in the Resurrection? Have I ever had any doubts that Jesus truly died, and therefore truly rose from the dead? Though the women weren't afraid to follow and discover where Jesus had been laid, where were the disciples? The sexual stereotypes that we assume about people weren't valid even then. Do I still stereotype women and men?

MARK 15:42-47

▼

MARK 16:1-8	What difference does the Resurrection make in my life right now? What difference does the fact that Jesus rose from the dead make in my relationship with my parents, my girlfriend, my boyfriend, my job, my school life? Putting it another way, would my life be different if someone proved that the Resurrection didn't happen?

▼

MARK 16:9-13	The apostles obviously doubted Mary as well as the two companions who saw Jesus while traveling out of town. Why? Have I ever doubted the faith experiences of others? How do I decide whether the faith experiences of others are valid?

▼

MARK 16:14-18	Though Jesus appeared to the 11 disciples after he had appeared to several others, and though he scolded them for their unbelief, did Jesus yet rely on them and trust them with his mission to the world? Will Jesus trust me even when I fail him repeatedly, when my belief is weak? Has Jesus also sent me out to share his love and his Word with others? What signs of his power does God give believers today so that they can more effectively share his message?

▼

MARK 16:19-20	Do I really understand that Jesus is alive and well for me right now? Do I realize that he can help me now? Do I believe that he will not only work alongside of me, but confirm that reality to me each day?

The Gospel According to

LUKE

▼

Though written down by one man, the Gospel according to Luke was compiled from accounts by several eyewitnesses. Does that help me realize how trustworthy the Bible is?	LUKE 1:1-4

▼

Zechariah was a religious man—yet he was still blown away when God answered his prayer. When I pray to God, do I actually believe that God will answer my prayer, or would I be as surprised as Zechariah? God said that John the Baptist would be a "joy and delight"—but John was considered weird by most, and was eventually beheaded. Not exactly the joy and delight one would have in mind. What, then, made John a joy and delight? Would I be willing to do what it takes to be a joy and delight to God?	LUKE 1:5-17

▼

Zechariah's doubts robbed him of his speech. Do doubts about my faith cripple my attempts to share with others the good news of Christ? Elizabeth's inability to bear a child made her feel inadequate—yet God removed her inadequacy. What are my inadequacies? Do I believe that God can take them away?	LUKE 1:18-25

▼

If I became miraculously pregnant while still unmarried, would I consider it a blessing from God? Although the angel announced that Mary would be the mother of Jesus, Mary	LUKE 1:26-38

could have refused the offer. Yet she said yes. How many things that God has promised me remain unfulfilled because I haven't said yes to God?

▼

**LUKE
1:39-45**

Elizabeth recognized that Mary's role in God's plan was more important than her own, submitting to Mary's greater blessing without envying her. Can I rejoice with others when they achieve what I can't achieve?

▼

**LUKE
1:46-56**

Did I read this prayer carefully? It is a moving yet radical prayer. "He has scattered those who are proud"—what does that mean? Or what about "He has brought down the rulers from their thrones" or "He has lifted up the humble...but has sent the rich away empty"? Are these promises to be fulfilled in the future, or is God fulfilling them right now?

▼

**LUKE
1:57-66**

Even when we specifically ask God to do things and he does them, we tend to explain them away as coincidence or chance. Zechariah didn't. Have I, though? Zechariah obeyed God and immediately received his speech back. When I obey God, does it give me more confidence to speak genuinely and effectively about my faith?

▼

**LUKE
1:67-80**

Here is a genuine prayer of gratitude and praise. Have I ever prayed to God this kind of prayer? What am I grateful to God for? Although praising God the way Zechariah did sounds kind of weird, what things could I say to God that acknowledge all the good things about him? Do I try to praise God each day?

▼

**LUKE
2:1-7**

Do I realize that God was fulfilling prophecy by working through a pagan emperor? Do I realize that God is working right now in the world, even though I can't see or understand all that he's doing? Jesus was born into poverty and simplicity. Does that say something about the way I should live my life?

▼

LUKE
2:8-20

Why did God send his heavenly messengers to poor, simple, powerless shepherds instead of to the religious leaders? Since God obviously knew what he was doing, why do I think the shepherds were more able to believe than the powerful religious leaders? Is my faith more like the faith of the shepherds or of the religious leaders? Do I respond more to glittering, glamorous money and power than to quiet, simple faith? In other words, would I be more excited about visiting the president of the United States or Mother Teresa?

▼

LUKE
2:21-24

Even though Jesus was God, he was still named, circumcised, and presented in the Temple according to the customs of Judaism. What does that say about my relationship with my church? Do I need the church? How can I respond to the laws of the church and still retain my personal relationship with God?

▼

LUKE
2:25-32

Because Simeon was actively seeking God's will, he immediately recognized Jesus as the Savior. Am I actively looking for God's will in my life? If I am, will I be better able to see Jesus in others? And just how do I go about finding God's will? By praying? Attending church? Reading my Bible?

▼

LUKE
2:33-38

Am I willing to accept the inevitable: that if I follow Christ, I will experience sorrow and sacrifice as well as joy and peace? Do I realize that good always exposes the bad and that truth always illuminates falsehood? Is my faith strong enough to believe the truth even when it attracts ugliness and hostility?

▼

LUKE 2:39-52

Do I realize that sometimes there will be conflict between God's will and the wishes of my parents? How did Jesus resolve this conflict? What conflicts might arise in my own life because of a difference in God's seeming will for me and what my parents want for me?

▼

LUKE 3:1-9, 15-22

Now that I've read the words of Isaiah the prophet (vv. 4-6), what mountains of bad habits, bad actions, bad attitudes, or bad influences do I have to tear down and get rid of? Why did John speak harshly to those who listened to him? Is there anything in me that I have the feeling I should quit, but haven't felt that God cares one way or the other? Why can't I quit before God is harsh with me?

▼

LUKE 3:10-14

Can I follow John the Baptist's commands? Am I generous to those who are less fortunate? Am I careful not to misuse my influence, whether on boyfriends, girlfriends, or friends at school or church? Have I ever thought of myself as greedy? What does it mean to be greedy? Am I capable of being greedy?

▼

LUKE 3:23-38

Here's another list of Jesus' ancestors, similar to the one in the beginning of Matthew's Gospel—but only similar, not identical. Matthew traces the ancestry of Jesus as far back as Abraham—how far back does Luke go? Why? Matthew begins his genealogy with Abraham and works his way up to Jesus, chronologically. In what order does Luke list the Messiah's relatives? Why?

▼

Jesus was tempted to use his powers to please, to entertain, to capture the crowd's attention—yet he refused to do any of these things. Why? Does that tell me anything about how I should make decisions? Does it suggest that if I or anyone else draws large crowds and captures the world's attention, something might be inappropriate if not wrong? Am I able to decide what to do without thinking about how my friends and family are going to react?

LUKE
4:1-13

▼

It sounds like the presence of Jesus in the world has not only personal consequences (peace, joy, forgiveness), but social consequences as well. What are those consequences? What does that mean for me? Does God the Father want me to help today's victims of society? Can I find those at school who fit those categories? Can I find them in my town or neighborhood?

LUKE
4:14-21

**LUKE
4:22-30**

Have I taken my faith for granted? Have I taken for granted my freedom to believe in God and practice that belief? Do some who have grown up outside the Christian faith hunger more for God than I do? Have I become so familiar with my religion and my faith that it no longer influences or directs me?

▼

**LUKE
4:31-39**

In the synagogue Jesus commanded the powers of evil to come out of a possessed man. Then Jesus commanded sickness to leave Simon Peter's mother-in-law.

Do I turn to Jesus when I am troubled with sickness or with temptations from the powers of evil? Do I follow Christ's example by helping my friends when they are tempted to do wrong? Do I pray for and visit friends of mine when they are ill?

▼

**LUKE
4:40-44**

After Jesus healed the man in the synagogue and Peter's mother-in-law, many more sick people were brought to Jesus. He refused none of them, but worked all night long healing them. But at dawn when he went off alone to pray, the people pursued him, asking him to stay. Jesus refused. Do I realize that, at times, I can help people as much by saying no as by saying yes? How do I know when to say yes and when to say no?

▼

**LUKE
5:1-11**

Has God acted as powerfully in me as he did in the apostles when he invited them to follow him? Has God invited me to follow him? How have I responded to his call in my life? How would I like to respond in the future?

▼

**LUKE
5:12-16**

The leper knew Jesus could make him whole again, and Jesus did make him whole. What things in my life are coming apart right now? Can God make me whole again if I ask him?

The friends of the paralyzed man brought him to Christ. Am I trying to bring my friends to Christ? Do I really believe that Christ can heal, forgive, and make my friends' lives better? How much do I believe it?

LUKE 5:17-26

▼

Jesus reached out to sinners and ate with them. First he accepted them as they were—and then, in love and only gradually, he challenged them to change.

Has my experience of Christ and his Church been deep enough and strong enough for me to endure the sacrifices of sharing his work? Am I strong enough to mix with and reach out to hardened sinners in order to bring them to Christ, or do I still need to grow more in my faith so I won't be led astray and fall into their sins myself?

LUKE 5:27-35

▼

Jesus was dressing humanity in a new coat—he was offering us new wine. That is, he had for us a new set of values that would fulfill and complete God's plan for us. The Pharisees and other Jewish leaders, therefore, became upset, for they wanted things to stay just like they were. They wanted everyone to be satisfied with old coats and old wine—like they were.

Do I realize that when I personally accept Jesus into my heart, I become a new person (2 Cor. 5:17) and accept new standards and values that are very different from those of most kids today? Do I realize that if I try to live out my faith, I'll probably upset many of my friends just as Jesus did? When I find my beliefs upsetting others, what will I do? Change what I believe, keep quiet, or continue to stand firm and take whatever consequences come my way?

LUKE 5:36- 6:11

▼

LUKE 6:12-26

Jesus was an incredibly charismatic teacher, for thousands were attracted to his teaching. Why did people listen to him? When I go to church or Sunday school or confirmation, is it boring? Why? What could my minister or priest or teacher learn from Jesus?

▼

LUKE 6:27-36

Does Jesus actually want me to love all my enemies? Is it easier to love enemies I don't know than it is to love the ones who have personally attacked me? Is it even possible to love those who would harm me? If I turn the other cheek, will my enemy take advantage of my kindness?

I've always heard in church that if I show kindness to my enemies, it will cause them to respect me and back off—yet Jesus ended up getting killed by his enemies. How can I find the strength to love my enemies even when they use my love against me?

▼

LUKE 6:37-42

Before I criticize someone else for a fault, do I ask myself if there are reasons for their behavior that I don't know about? Do I ask myself if I've ever been guilty of the same kinds of things?

▼

LUKE 6:43-45

If someone were to judge me by my fruits, what would they conclude about me? Do my good fruits outweigh my bad fruits?

▼

LUKE 6:46-49

How have the last few weeks of studying the New Testament helped the foundation of my life? This parable has to do with acting on Jesus' words instead of merely reading them. What efforts have I made so far to practice what I've been reading? What can I do starting now?

▼

Jesus honored the faith of a man who didn't fit into all the right categories: he was a Roman centurion, an officer of the occupying army, a slave owner, very wealthy—and he was a very good man. In fact, when his daughter was healed, Jesus commented that he had not found such great faith even in Israel.

   Am I willing to admit that true Christians may not hold the political views I do, or be in the same economic class I'm in, or agree with all my opinions? Am I willing to see through the external differences and respond to our common faith?

Though this was a spectacular miracle, why did Jesus do it? Because it was spectacular and caused everyone to be awed with his power and authority, or because he was moved with compassion? Do I realize that Jesus sometimes did things that alienated the crowds, and then at other times caused them to be astonished? Yet whether crowds were alienated or astonished, it didn't matter to Jesus—for he was unconcerned with the crowd's response. Am I cultivating this trait in my own life?

Jesus and John the Baptist were very different from each other, but both had a call and a mission from God. Do I sometimes criticize those who are called differently than me? Do I sometimes make my calling the basis for excluding anyone different from myself?

Have I ever had a debt cancelled? Have I ever received forgiveness from someone I had expected revenge and retaliation from? I know God's done that for me—but do I really feel his forgiveness? Do I need to stop for a minute and think about the debt that he cancelled and the forgiveness he continually gives to me?

LUKE
8:1-3

The Church needs money to operate and minister. The work of Christ requires much money. Do I feel any responsibility to provide some of that money? Am I willing to let my faith affect even my finances—like the women who followed Jesus?

▼

LUKE
8:4-15

Do I remember this parable when I plant seeds of faith in others? Do I realize that some will reject me or immediately forget what I've done because the ground has not been prepared? Others will accept it but then lose interest. Others will accept it but then be led away by temptation. Others, however, will accept it and nourish it—and they will blossom and grow.

Do I realize that in the four cases where the seed failed to survive, it was good seed that was planted? It was the same faith that bloomed in another. The difference lies in the attitude and actions of those who receive it.

Can this knowledge keep me from doubt or despair when those around me do not believe, or when they reject my advice or the faith I share with them? Can this parable help me remember that it's not me (the planter) who's failed in such circumstances, nor is it weakness in my faith (the seed)? Do I understand that the failure instead is due to the receptivity and commitment of those with whom I share my faith?

▼

Do I hide my faith? How do I hide my faith from others? Is Jesus saying that if I share my faith openly, it will be strengthened; and that if I hide my faith, what faith I have will be diminished?

LUKE 8:16-21

▼

The disciples panicked during the storm because they assumed Jesus didn't care. Have there been crises in my life when God was silent and I wondered if he even cared? What did this event teach me about God's caring when I'm in stormy waters? When Jesus acted, the disciples became even more afraid. How do I distinguish being afraid of God from fearing God? Do I fear God? Should I fear God?

LUKE 8:22-25

▼

Do I believe I can call upon Jesus when I'm bothered by serious anger, hatred, and lust? What are the demons in my life? Do I believe Christ can rid me of them? When I am helped by God, do I share what he's done in my life with others, or do I keep it to myself? Am I afraid that if I talk too much about what God is doing in me, my friends and family might

LUKE 8:26-39

reject me just as the townspeople rejected the demon-possessed man? Do I realize that sometimes people don't want me to get better, they don't want me to fix my problems—because then I'd threaten them?

▼

LUKE 8:40-56

Compare the faith of the woman who touched Jesus' clothes with the faith of Jairus and his friends. Am I more like the woman, who believed she could be healed by mere contact with Jesus even when he didn't intentionally try to heal her? Or am I more like Jairus and his friends, who thought that Jesus could heal sickness only if he were right there, standing over the person to be healed?

This woman had been sick for 12 years before she was healed. Do I sometimes expect Jesus to produce instant results for me? Do I become frustrated if he doesn't? How can I learn to wait on God?

▼

LUKE 9:1-6

When I communicate my faith and my friends do not welcome me, how do I "shake the dust off my feet"? How does my relationship with my friends make me react to their negative response? If strangers reject me because of my faith, do I respond differently than if my friends reject my faith?

▼

LUKE 9:7-9

Although he had taken care of John the Baptist, Herod was still confused. Why? God's power was still alive and present in the world. Have I ever been confused by the strong evidence of God's power today—miracles, healings, speaking in tongues? Do I casually write all those things off as "weird"—or do I look into them to determine which ones are real and which ones are phony? Do I simply avoid or ignore what I don't understand?

▼

Do I believe that Jesus fed 5,000 people with a mere handful of fish and bread? Do I believe that Jesus can feed me what I need to live a satisfying Christian life today?

▼

Peter declared Jesus as the Messiah—and then Jesus told him that the Messiah would be no powerful earthly leader, but a powerless, persecuted leader. Jesus didn't stop there, either—he continued to tell Peter that all who follow him, including me, will be powerless and persecuted. We'll all carry crosses.

Do I believe that? Am I willing to be powerless, to be persecuted, to carry a cross—all this in order to follow Jesus? Do I believe that persecution and crosses are necessary to my Christian growth and maturity?

▼

Often God clearly and dramatically demonstrates his presence and power in order to strengthen our faith and give us courage for difficult times. Am I like Peter, who wanted to remain on the mountaintop and keep receiving the powerful presence of God instead of going down the mountain and continuing God's work?

When the disciples returned from the mountain, they discovered that their wonderful experience on the mountain was no shortcut to a deeper life. Although the camps, retreats, and inspirational events I attend seem so rich at the time, do I often forget all about them only a few days later? Do I realize that great experiences never take the place of work and discipline in my Christian life?

▼

The disciples still did not understand that Jesus would suffer persecution and death because they were still counting on him to install them in positions of power. Do I understand how difficult it is to follow Christ and give up claims to power and prestige? Do I truly understand that to follow Jesus will always put me out of step with my culture?

▼

LUKE 9:49-56

Does Christ want me to rejoice in the good deeds and worthwhile accomplishments of others—even if these others hurt or reject me?

▼

LUKE 9:57-62

What stipulations have I put on following God's invitations to me? What excuses have I used to avoid following Christ's call to me?

▼

LUKE 10:1-24

Jesus chose 72 more followers and sent them out in the same way he did earlier (Luke 9:1-10). They came back full of joy, having experienced the power of Jesus in their lives. Have I ever experienced the power of God in my life? Have I ever felt Jesus working in me? What would it take for me to experience what the 72 disciples experienced?

▼

LUKE 10:25-37

How can I be a true neighbor to others, especially to those I don't know?

▼

LUKE 10:38-42

Have I always thought that to be busy helping others for the Lord's sake is good? Do I really agree with what Jesus told Martha? How do I know when to serve God actively and when to stop working, sit down, and listen to him?

▼

LUKE 11:1-13

Has the Lord's Prayer become meaningless to me because I have said it so many times? Can I pray the Lord's Prayer and mean it? Do I believe that God loves me like a Father? Do I believe that God will send nothing my way that would be ultimately disastrous to me? Can he give me enough grace and strength to resist temptation and stand firm in trials?

▼

Do I take evil seriously? Does evil frighten me? Do I really believe that God has power over the devil and his evil forces in this world? Do I take evil seriously enough to realize that I am constantly exposed to evil forces and evil people in my life? Do I ask God to help me overcome the evil in my life?

LUKE 11:14-22

▼

Do I realize that not choosing to follow Christ is choosing to not follow Christ? Do I realize that making no decision is essentially deciding? Do I realize that every day of my life I am put in the position of either choosing to follow Christ or choosing to reject him? And do I realize that life is not static—that every day I am moving either towards God or away from him? Which way am I moving now?

LUKE 11:23-28

LUKE 11:29-32

Am I aware of the double meaning Jesus intended in comparing himself with Jonah? Jonah, remember, gave the people of Ninevah no sign or miracle beyond his strong preaching—and neither would he, stated Jesus. Furthermore, as Jonah was three days in the big fish and survived, so also Jesus would be three days in the tomb and rise again.

Because I know that Jesus did rise again and still lives today, do I therefore follow his preaching as recorded in the Gospels much more closely than did the people of his time? In what ways do I and in what ways do I not?

▼

LUKE 11:33-36

Do my eyes lead me into temptation, into sin, or into even the neighborhood of sin? Do the movies I see, for example, the videos I watch, and the magazines I read cause me to think sexual thoughts that I'm better off not thinking? Worse, do they desensitize me to the effects of what I see so that I tolerate sin in me and justify it by thinking that, since everyone else does it, it must not be wrong?

Do I take sin seriously, or do I figure that it really doesn't matter since I can always ask for forgiveness? Do I realize that when I tolerate sin in my life, it changes me and makes me able to tolerate even more sin?

▼

LUKE 11:37-54

What things would Jesus criticize in my life right now? Am I at all hypocritical in my faith? Am I willing to listen to criticism and then make the changes in me I need to make?

▼

LUKE 12:1-7

Am I more conscious of physical danger to me than I am of spiritual danger? What are some spiritual dangers that I face right now? Do I believe that God will take care of me and of my ultimate well-being just as he takes care of the sparrows?

Do I realize that if I live a secret Christianity and refuse to publicly claim Christ by my words and actions, Christ says he will be unable to claim me at the last judgment? Does this heavy penalty apply if I just occasionally hold back from claiming Christ when I should, or only if I consistently deny Christ and eliminate him altogether from my life?

What role does the Holy Spirit play in all of this? Could the "unforgivable sin" mean that if I deliberately refuse to seek God, I will never find him and therefore live out the consequences of my decision? How can I keep myself open to the Holy Spirit in my everyday life?

LUKE 12:8-12

▼

Like the rich fool, do I get so caught up in my material plans and worldly activities that I forget about eternal and spiritual realities? If I were to die tonight, would I be ready to meet my God? What can I do to keep myself always ready to meet God? Do I sometimes live as if the purpose of life was simply to "eat, drink and be merry"? What is the purpose of my life?

LUKE 12:13-21

▼

Do I trust that God will help me get what I need—and believe that anything else is unnecessary? Do I worry about my future plans, or do I trust that God will lead me where he wants me to be and that I will be happy with his decision? Do I put more importance on my plans and desires for the future and for material things than on his plans and will for me?

LUKE 12:22-31

▼

Do we grow closer to God when we give up our own possessions and wealth for the sake of the poor and of those who are in need? Is growing closer to God more important to me than my material possessions? Am I eager to

LUKE 12:32-40

use my possessions and my talents for others instead of only for myself? Is my attachment to my possessions flexible enough that I'd be able to give them up at a moment's notice if God came to me in prayer or through some other sign and asked me to give them up for his sake?

▼

LUKE 12:41-48

Though I know God sees everything I do, do I still act as if God were not watching me? How can I try to become more aware of his presence?

▼

LUKE 12:49-53

Is my Christian commitment an element of unity or division within my own family? Is there anything I can do, short of compromising my faith, to make things better? Are the differences within my family genuinely spiritual in nature, or are our difficulties simply the typical problems of growing up and adjusting to each other?

▼

LUKE 12:54-59

Jesus talked a lot about signs. Do I recognize God's signs in my life? Do I know how to find his will for me? Do I hear his warnings? When I have differences with a friend, do I try to resolve the issue myself, or do I use the "courts"—that is, my friends or other people?

▼

LUKE 13:1-5

Am I aware that the kind of death that Jesus is warning me about here is spiritual death, eternal death, a life forever without God? Do I ever think about this consequence of sin? If I did more often, would it help me turn away from sin?

▼

LUKE 13:6-9

Do I realize how important I am in the kingdom of God? Do I realize that the fruit, or gifts, that I have to offer are necessary and important for God's work to multiply?

What are my gifts? Am I bearing fruit for the kingdom of God? Do I appreciate the wonderful mercy of God, who—like the gardener—gives me another chance to bear fruit? Is it also possible that "fruits" refers to the visible results of Christ being present in my life—things like love, patience, kindness, peace, joy?

▼

Jesus didn't let rules get in the way of his compassion. Do I let the rules of peer pressure get in the way of my befriending and having compassion for the school nerd, the brain, the "retard," or another unpopular person? Does that loving compassion lead me to befriend them and defend them, thus working against the unjust peer pressure that hurts them and discriminates against them?

LUKE 13:10-17

▼

Does it seem that those who do not fit into our materialistic American culture because of their Christian commitment have little status or importance in this life? Do I realize how little good it takes to make a real difference in the world? Does it encourage me to know that whatever I do for God will be multiplied and increased? Like the narrow door, do I feel the narrowness of my commitment to Christ? What does that narrowness look like?

LUKE 13:18-30

▼

Do I admire Jesus for not being afraid of Herod? In fact, he seemed to fear nothing. What am I afraid of? Can Jesus help me become less afraid? Was it easier for Jesus because he was God, or did he battle with fear just like I do? Even though Jesus knew he would be killed at the hands of the very people he now ministered to, he felt only sorrow and compassion for them. How am I towards those who reject or speak against me? How do I

LUKE 13:31-35

learn to see beyond what people do, and try instead to understand why they do it?

▼

LUKE 14:1-11

Am I like the Pharisees, who were so wrapped up in where they sat around the meal table that they overlooked the man who was ill? Do I often get so wrapped up in my activity that I don't have a clue to the needs of my friends? Do I ignore those who are unpopular, those who aren't part of my group of friends? Do I pass by those whom I have no need of, even though they might have needs that I can fill?

▼

LUKE 14:12-14

When I do something good, do I expect to be paid back by those I have helped? When I decide to help someone, do I consider what I'll receive in return? If my only reward in heaven is for those deeds for which I receive no return or no thanks, how much reward can I look forward to?

What kinds of excuses do I think up that keep me from following Christ seriously? What excuses do I use when I know that I should pray or read my Bible? What does this parable teach me? What am I going to do differently because of this parable?

▼

Have I counted the cost of following Christ? Have I systematically thought about the cost of discipleship in my love life? My dating life? My family? My friends? My vocation? My economic status? My future plans? What does Christ mean when he says that if I am not willing to give up everything, I cannot be his disciple? What does he mean by "everything"? When Jesus talks about salt losing its saltiness, what does he mean? Does he mean that if my commitment to Christ has no visible results, then I should question the depth of my commitment?

▼

Who can I relate to best: the lost sheep, the lost coin, the lost son, or one who rejoices when the lost is found? That is, do I see myself more as a recipient of Jesus' daily mercy, or as one who cooperates with Jesus in bringing his mercy, forgiveness, and guidance to others? The lost son was not merely a bit misguided—he deliberately and intentionally turned his back on his father and sinned greatly. He squandered his father's money and failed morally—yet he came back to his father expecting nothing.

When I sin, do I really expect to be forgiven, especially if it isn't the first time I have sinned in a certain way? Can I understand why the older brother was angry? Wouldn't I have been angry also? Which was more difficult—returning to one's father and admitting failure, or forgiving one's son for his failure? Did I notice that, in all three parables—after the coin, the sheep, and the son were found—there was a celebration, a party? Do I realize how many parties God has thrown in my behalf?

▼

LUKE 16:1-12

This is a very strange parable (it's puzzled even the best of theologians). Jesus used an example of dishonesty (embezzling, lying, etc.) to make a moral lesson. What was Jesus saying? Is he condoning immoral behavior, or merely using it as an example? Is he suggesting that Christians need to become shrewder business people? Or is he, as some commentators say, commending the man's foresight rather than his dishonesty? What did I learn from this parable?

▼

LUKE 16:13-18

How can money be an obstacle to following God? Do I control my money or does my money control me? Is it possible to have lots of money and not be controlled by it? Does Jesus control my money?

And what about what Jesus said about divorce? Do I agree with his difficult teaching about the lifelong commitment in marriage?

▼

LUKE 16:19-31

Have I ever neglected someone who really needed my help—and I knew it? Do I respond to people according to how they look on the exterior, or do I respond to the interior of people? Jesus says that even if a person rose from the dead and returned to the living in order to warn his friends of the fate that awaited them, they would not change their lives. What impact has the resurrection of Christ had on my life?

▼

LUKE 17:1-6

Am I aware how terrible it is to lead others into sin or evil through my bad example? Am I aware how terrible it is to confuse my friends with statements like "It isn't really that wrong" or "Everyone does it"? Do I take seriously the power of my influence on others? How many of my friends do I significantly influence? Am I able to forgive others even when I consider them a bad influence on me or my friends?

▼

What is Jesus saying in this strange passage? The reason it's strange to us may be because it speaks of duty. When I follow God, do I expect him to appreciate what I've done? Or do I understand that, because God is God, whatever I do is my duty—only what I was expected to do? Do I realize that it is always in my best interest as a creature to follow the designs of my Creator—and that should be all the reward I need?

"It may be possible to satisfy the claims of the law," writes a commentator about this passage, "but every lover knows that nothing he or she can ever do can satisfy the claims of love." What do I think of this statement?

LUKE 17:7-10

▼

Like the Samaritan leper, do I ever take time to stop and thank God for all he's given me? Is there any reason why I can't do that right now? Can I make a list of things God has given me and then refer to that list daily, adding new things as I think of them?

LUKE 17:11-19

▼

Does this passage make me nervous? When I hear about Jesus interrupting history and returning and surprising people in the normal activities of a day, does that worry me? If Jesus came back this very minute, would I be ready to meet him? If not, what would I have to do to get ready? Do I really believe that if I "lose my life" by giving up things I want, I will gain more now and in the life to come? Do I really believe Christ is coming back—even, perhaps, in my lifetime? If I believe that, do I live like I believe it?

LUKE 17:20-37

LUKE 18:1-8

Do I have the faith of the persistent widow? Am I willing to pray to God about certain needs for as long as it takes to get an answer from him—or do I place time limits on God's answers? Do I really believe that God is a just God? Do I really trust the justice of God? In other words, do I believe that someday, when all the accounts are settled, that all of us—including me—will be treated justly and fairly?

▼

LUKE 18:9-17

Am I aware of the danger of spiritual pride? Does my desire to serve God make me feel superior to those who have less desire to serve him? How can I keep that from happening? What's good about recognizing how sinful I am? How can that recognition help my relationship with God and with others?

▼

LUKE 18:18-30

Am I like the rich man in my attachment to material things? Does my desire for material things keep me from God? How much time do I spend shopping or just thinking about shopping or planning my next shopping trip? Why does God point out that it is easier for the poor to serve God than the rich? Why do poor people often need God, while the rich often feel self-sufficient?

Do I honestly believe that if I give up material things for the sake of God, I will gain not only riches in heaven but also things of much greater value here on earth? What practical things could I do right now with my money that would help me understand what God means? (Sponsor a child, help someone in need, etc.)

▼

LUKE 18:31-34

Why didn't the apostles understand Jesus when he spoke about the necessity of his suffering and death? When I read passages promising suffering and possibly death for me if I follow Christ, do I really believe he means me? Do I expect suffering because I follow Christ? Am I suffering now? Or do I work to avoid suffering for my faith?

▼

In his attempt to get Jesus' attention so that he could be healed, the blind man had to out-yell many who tried to shut him up and keep him from bothering Jesus. When I'm feeling blind spiritually and I need to go to Jesus, do I too easily give in to the tendency to instead get a good night's sleep or talk to a friend or wait to see if things will get better on their own? Or do I push on to Jesus even when my friends or family try to discourage me and act like they're threatened by my relationship with Christ? How badly do I want to see things the way Jesus does? How badly do I want the kind of spiritual discernment Jesus had?

LUKE 18:35-43

LUKE 19:1-10

Am I willing to exert extraordinary effort in order to be with Jesus? For example, do I try to get alone with Christ every day, even though it's hard to be alone? Do I try to spend time with Christ daily even though I'm busy? And when I do spend time with Jesus, am I willing to get rid of bad habits or friends, bad influences, material things—anything that keeps me from truly following Christ just like Zacchaeus?

▼

LUKE 19:11-27

Which of the three groups in this story do I fit into: the citizens who didn't want the nobleman to be king over them, the nobleman's two servants who used their talents and increased what the master gave to them, or the servant who refused to use the talents he had?

I have probably been in all three groups during different times in my life. Which group am I in now? How about my friends? At what times did I not want God to be king of my life? How did I overcome that attitude? When have I been afraid to use my gifts for God? When did I ignore my responsibility and feign ignorance? How did I overcome that attitude? And when have I really wanted to invest my life and my gifts for God's kingdom? How can I multiply those times?

▼

LUKE 19:28-40

Have I ever experienced the joy of recognition and approval from my friends for following Christ, whether at church camp, at school, or in my home? Ignoring the frowns of the religious leaders, the entire welcoming crowd cheered Christ—but a few days later, the crowd joined the Pharisees in demanding Christ's crucifixion.

What does that tell me about crowds? What does it tell me about recognition and approval from crowds? How do I learn to listen more to the approval of Christ and less to the approval of others—even if those others are people I respect?

▼

Do I have the attitude of Christ towards my enemies? Is it actually possible not only to lose my fear of my enemies, but to learn to view them with compassion instead of hatred? In other words, can I look, as Jesus does, not at their behavior, but at the reasons for their behavior? Yet at the same time, do I have the courage to stand up to my enemies and confront them when they do evil, as Christ did when he stood up against the moneychangers in the temple? It's one thing to follow Christ before I know what it costs—but after I've realized the cost I'll pay, do I have the courage to keep following Christ?

LUKE 19:41-48

▼

Do I realize that when people are critical of me, they sometimes ask difficult questions just to harass me and not because they want an answer? The issue of authority is significant. Do I believe that Jesus had God's authority? Do I really believe that when I follow Christ, I have authority? Do I understand that people recognize one with authority? When Mother Teresa walks into a room, she has authority. Everyone, including Senators and Heads of State can recognize it. Do I really understand that the closer I get to Christ the more his authority communicates through me to others?

LUKE 20:1-8

▼

The workers in the vineyard decided to take things into their own hands. They decided to ignore the owner of the vineyard, destroy his messengers, and manage the vineyard themselves. Am I like those workers? Do I constantly ignore the messengers of God in my life and do my own thing? Do I kill Christ by rejecting his words in my life?

LUKE 20:9-18

LUKE 20:19-26

Do I "render to Caesar what is rightfully Caesar's"? Do I obey the laws of our society? But do I also understand that, in a society that increasingly ignores God, there may be unjust or immoral laws that I cannot obey? Am I willing to resist the government at those times? Do I have the courage to follow God's law rather than human law?

▼

LUKE 20:27-40

Do I believe in heaven? If I do, do I look forward to going there? Do I realize that my relationships with friends will be totally different from what they are here on earth—and yet at the same time as wonderfully close and rich? What do I think Jesus meant when he said, "He is not the God of the dead, but of the living, for to him all are alive"?

▼

LUKE 20:41-21:4

When I act like a fine Christian at church and then live totally the opposite when I'm with my friends or at school—at times like these, do I resemble the Pharisees who paraded around in their religion? When I talk about religious things, do I share the truth or do I mouth only what people want to hear or expect me to say? Do I realize that Jesus knows absolutely everything about me and still loves me? Do I realize that, because of this, it is not the greatness of the things I do or the amount of things I do for the Lord that count, but simply that I do all I can for him—just as the poor widow gave all she had?

▼

LUKE 21:5-6

Jesus predicted that the Temple, the symbol of God's commitment to the Jewish people, would not be permanent. His prediction came true within 40 years. Do I realize that many of the things I believe are permanent actually aren't? Do I trust completely the permanence of God?

Have I ever known one who fits this description of a false prophet—someone who says he is teaching what Christ says, but instead is distorting what Christ says? Can a priest or a minister or a TV evangelist or a teacher or a boyfriend or girlfriend ever be a false prophet? How can I tell if someone is a false prophet? What does Jesus tell me to do if I think someone is a false prophet?

LUKE 21:7-8

▼

Jesus says that earthquakes, famines, and plagues are allowed by him. Does that bother me? When it's a friend or loved one hit by a natural disaster, this teaching is hard to swallow. What is the difference between believing that God allows things to happen and that he makes things happen? Which do I believe?

LUKE 21:9-19

▼

Jesus used the image of the destruction of Jerusalem to talk about his second coming at the end of the world and our personal moment of judgment at our death. When I read this, do I feel hopeful or fearful? Why? What is Christian hope? Does it mean I get out of all the bad stuff at the end of the world, or does it mean that whatever happens, Christ will overcome in the end?

LUKE 21:20-36

▼

Judas betrayed Jesus by exploiting their friendship. Have I ever betrayed a close friend by sharing a confidence or betraying a trust? Have I ever apologized for that betrayal and tried to restore the friendship? Have I ever been betrayed by a close friend? How did I feel? Can I forgive him or her? Have I forgiven?

    The Jewish leaders and Judas wanted to capture Jesus privately, without the public knowing. Am I involved in something now that no one knows about and that I assume

LUKE 21:37-22:6

will be okay as long as no one finds out? Intellectually I know God knows everything—but does that really make any difference?

▼

LUKE 22:7-20

Do I look forward to Holy Communion or the Eucharist? Do I feel close to Jesus when I partake of Communion? Do I believe that the ceremony of Holy Communion or Eucharist is a special occasion in which Jesus is present differently than at any other occasion? How long has it been since I have partaken of Holy Communion or Eucharist?

▼

LUKE 22:21-24

The disciples were shocked that one of them might betray Jesus—only to turn around and argue among themselves about who would be the greatest in the kingdom. Do I realize how dangerous my selfishness and pride are?

My pride can blind me to my wrong-doing, and then cause me to become outraged when it's pointed out to me. Am I willing to admit that I am very capable of betraying Christ? Am I willing to own up to the sin in my life right now?

▼

Jesus makes it crystal clear that his followers are to be servants. Do I really believe that? How am I a servant? How important is service in my life? Am I constantly looking for ways to serve others? How could I serve others in my life right now?

LUKE 22:25-30

▼

Simon Peter assumed that he was strong enough on his own to avoid temptation. He felt totally adequate to live the Christian life on his own. Have I ever felt that way? Do I feel that way now? Why does it so often take a personal crisis for me to realize how inadequate I am?

LUKE 22:31-34

▼

Jesus spoke in a parable about the need for spiritual strength and courage. The apostles misunderstood him—they took his comment literally, thinking they should go out and get real swords. Jesus told them to stop talking like that. When one of them did use a sword, Jesus again asked them to stop. The disciples' misunderstanding was probably predictable, for the Jews expected the Messiah to come with physical force and crush the Romans—yet Jesus himself was crushed by the Romans.

LUKE 22:35-38,49-51

What does this passage teach me about real power? Why do I always want to rely on physical force instead of spiritual force? Do I really believe in spiritual force? Do I honestly trust in the power of God rather than in the power of men?

▼

LUKE 22:39-44

Jesus told the apostles to pray so that they would not fall into temptation. Then he practiced what he preached and prayed to the Father even as he was overcome with great fear at what was about to happen because of the consequences of his mission.

Do I realize that Jesus endured the same kind of weakness and temptation that I go through? When I feel weak or when God's will seems unattractive, painful, or frightening, do I turn to God as Jesus did? Jesus' prayer was answered and he was strengthened by an angel. Have I ever been strengthened against temptation or encouraged to do God's will as a result of prayer?

▼

LUKE 22:45-48,52-62

For the second time, Jesus told the apostles to pray so that they would not fall into temptation—but they slept instead. Then, even after witnessing the terrible sin of Judas' betrayal, they all sinned that night in practically the same way by abandoning or denying Christ.

When I neglect prayer and time with God, do I become as weak as the apostles were that night? Do I fall into temptation and sin more easily? Do I concentrate on the sins or shortcomings of others when my own sins and faults are just as bad?

▼

LUKE 22:63-71

Jesus was mocked and beaten for the first time since his capture, then condemned by his own words for telling the truth about who he was. Do I realize that if I follow Christ and tell the truth, I will likely face persecution and condemnation instead of being rewarded? Am I fooled into expecting that truth will earn me respect and admiration instead of rejection and criticism? Why does the truth often hurt? Why does telling the truth often cause people to become hostile and defensive? Do I like to hear the truth, especially when it's about me?

When Pilate sent Jesus to Herod, Herod demanded that Jesus perform a miracle. Yet Jesus refused to cooperate with the murderer of John the Baptist, even though by doing so he would have saved his life. Am I tempted to compromise with evil people in order to gain favor or approval from them? Do I exploit my relationship with God for my momentary benefit, or do I ask the hard question: Is what I am doing benefiting the kingdom of God?

LUKE 23:1-12

▼

Pilate clearly tried to appease the crowd and appease his own conscience—for through it all, he didn't believe that Jesus was guilty of any crime. Yet his attempt to appease backfired. Do I try and walk that same line by trying to do both what God wants and what my friends want?

Does this passage teach me about decision making? When I make decisions, the first question I should ask should be, "What does God want me to do?" Can I allow that question to take precedence over all the other questions, like "What do my friends want me to do?" "What does my boyfriend or girlfriend want me to do?" "What do my parents want me to do?" "What do I want me to do?"

LUKE 23:13-25

▼

Simon was forced to help Jesus. Have there been times in my life when I have been forced to do the right thing, forced to encounter Jesus, forced to believe certain things—and then later discover that I benefited from that forced situation? When I feel bad about sin, is it usually because it hurts God or breaks his heart? But do I really understand that my sin always ends up hurting me? In what ways does sin hurt me?

LUKE 23:26-31

▼

Jesus showed patience, perseverance, courage, power, forgiveness, love, and endurance under the most cruel and painful of situations. What

LUKE 23:32-38

do I show under pressure? What does stress do to me? Can I learn from Jesus' example? Where can I find power, courage, forgiveness, love, and endurance when I'm under pressure or in pain?

▼

LUKE 23:39-46

One criminal wanted to use Jesus to get out of an unpleasant situation. The other criminal simply believed in Jesus because he was God. Where does my belief in God come from? Do I believe so I get from God what I want, or do I believe in God because he is God, because I believe he is the Truth?

▼

LUKE 23:47-56

If I had been one of Jesus' disciples, what would I have felt if the one I thought was the Savior and promised Messiah ended up arrested and killed? What do I feel when I pray for one who is sick or dying or otherwise in need—and nothing seems to happen? Have I ever thought that God was dead or inactive? Have I ever wondered just where God was?

▼

LUKE 24:1-12

The women—not the apostles—believed God's messengers at the tomb. In fact, the men didn't even take the time to go see the tomb for themselves, except for Peter.

Do I take time to learn, to pray, to "work out my own salvation" (Phil. 2:12)—in other words, to practice my faith daily? Or do I spend little effort, expecting instead that God will teach me everything I need to know? Am I willing to work at my faith? How could I put more effort into my faith?

▼

LUKE 24:13-32

The two disciples were so depressed because of the events of the previous days that they didn't recognize Jesus. When I get depressed and down, do I reject anyone and everyone who tries to help, including Jesus? Do I understand that although depression is a normal part of life, it can blind me to help that is right next to me? When I'm depressed, what can I do to prevent it from blinding me? What can I do for others who are depressed?

Can I remember a time when I've really made an effort to follow Christ? Was I rewarded by a special experience of God's presence? Do I imagine Jesus as some kind of ghost or spook, or do I believe that he was physically, bodily present in the flesh? Do I believe that Jesus was all man and all God? How important is it that I believe that Jesus was truly God and truly man?

LUKE 24:33-43

Jesus told the disciples that they would be the witnesses of who Jesus was. But he told them first to wait for the power of the Holy Spirit.

LUKE 24:44-49

We apparently have the same commission now as the disciples did then—we are to be his witnesses. Yet how do I witness to my friends that Jesus is alive and well in my life and in the world? Do I have the power of the Holy Spirit in my life? Do I even want that kind of power? Am I willing to ask God now for his Holy Spirit to empower me to be a witness of the truth of the living Christ to my family, to my friends, and to my world?

▼

LUKE 24:50-53

What happened to the disciples? Earlier, when Jesus was arrested and crucified, they were despondent and broken. Now Jesus leaves them again—yet this time they're joyful and happy. The disciples acquired courage, strength, power, authority, confidence, and joy from being with Jesus. How can I be with the living Jesus every day of my life?

The Gospel According to

JOHN

▼

John tells us here in the introduction to his narrative that Jesus was God, was with God in the beginning, and yet is the Son of God. What does that tell me about the Trinity? Jesus invaded human history with his life and light. How is Jesus life and light? Have I experienced the life and light of Jesus? Have I ever experienced the darkness of being without Christ? Why do I sometimes reject the light and head for the darkness? Why can darkness be so appealing?

JOHN 1:1-18

▼

Could I give as honest and accurate a description of myself and my mission as John the Baptist did? Can I openly admit, like John, what I am and what I'm not? Is it true that the more godly you are, the less godly you feel? Is it true that the closer I get to God, the further away from God I feel? John cared only that everything he did pointed to Jesus. Do I try and live like John?

JOHN 1:19-34

▼

After Andrew and Philip met Jesus, they hurried to tell Simon Peter (a relative) and Nathanael (a friend—see vv. 43-51) about him. Do I talk freely with my relatives and friends about my faith, about Jesus? Or do I hold back any mention of my faith or Jesus unless someone else brings it up?

JOHN 1:35-42

▼

JOHN
1:43-51

Jesus impressed Nathanael by his knowledge of him. Have I ever experienced the call of Christ in my life? Have I ever unquestionably heard God speaking to me through another person, through an experience, through the Bible, or simply in my mind? Do I seek God's presence? Do I ask for him to speak to me? Is it weird to ask God to somehow speak to me?

▼

JOHN
2:1-12

At the urging of his mother, Jesus performed an act of kindness to others—an act that revealed his powers and caused people to follow him. Do I realize how much of God's power is communicated through acts of kindness? Have I deliberately tried to show kindness to others? What acts of kindness could I do today to show God's power in my life?

▼

JOHN
2:13-25

The Jewish authorities and the people believed in Jesus only because he performed extra-ordinary acts and wonders. Have I demanded a sign from God in my life even though he has given me many signs in the past? Do I demand that God turns things out a certain way for me as proof that he loves me?

▼

JOHN
3:1-21

Why did Jesus say we had to be reborn? What did he mean? Have I been reborn? If not, what do I need to do? Can people be religious without being reborn? Can people be reborn without being religious?

▼

JOHN
3:22-36

John the Baptist came to introduce Christ to the world—but then he had to step aside. Has that ever happened to me, when someone else was chosen to finish what I started? Have I ever been irritated when someone else got credit for what I did? Can I ever get to the point where I don't care who gets the credit, as long as it points to Jesus?

▼

Jews were not to mix with Samaritans (v. 9), nor were Jewish men to talk with women in public (v. 27). But Jesus broke these barriers of prejudice. Following Jesus evidently means that I cannot be prejudiced. Do I have a problem with prejudice? Am I prejudiced against other races, against ethnic groups, against groups at school, against adults, the handicapped, the opposite sex? What can I do to be like Jesus—to rid myself of the last shred of prejudice?

JOHN
4:1-27

▼

The Samaritan woman had no problem talking about religion—but she was changed only when Jesus spoke to her hurts and needs. Do I tend to argue with people about my faith, or do I truly care about their hurts and their needs? Do I realize that arguments are often only smoke screens that cover up hurts and loneliness and spiritual need?

JOHN
4:28-30

▼

Have I ever tried to help someone who didn't listen and seemed not to care? Do I understand that God may want me sometimes to only plant the seed, but not harvest the full-grown crop? Do I realize that I am only one part of God's plan, and not the center of attention? Am I willing to accept the role of a planter and not just a harvester?

JOHN
4:31-38

▼

Do I realize that one sign of my growth in faith is that I believe Christ because of my first-hand experience with him, instead of merely hearing about another's experience with Christ? Am I seeking more first-hand experiences with Christ through my Bible reading and prayer?

JOHN
4:39-42

JOHN
4:43-44

Jesus said that "a prophet has no honor in his own country." What does that mean? Is my own family the hardest ones to convince of God's power in my life? Do I understand that, because they are so close to me and live with my faults, they may not see what God is doing? What can I do to overcome this?

▼

JOHN
4:45-54

When some were given a sign, it convinced them to believe in Christ. What signs can I remember in my life that convinced me that Jesus was who he said he was? Why did Jesus rebuke those who wanted signs—and then turn around and give signs to people who believed because of them?

▼

JOHN
5:1-18

"Do you want to get well again?" Jesus asked the man by the pool. What was behind Jesus' question? Are there some who actually don't want to get well? How does my desire to be healed affect Jesus' power to heal me? Is Jesus restrained from working in certain parts of me only because I don't want him to work there? What do I need to do about that?

▼

JOHN
5:19-47

Some people have a difficult time believing in Jesus. Sure, they believe there may well be a God—but Jesus? Is it difficult for me to believe in Jesus? Do I really believe Jesus is the Son of God? Why do I believe that Jesus is God—because of what I've read about him? Because of what he's done in my life? Because of what he's done in others' lives?

▼

JOHN
6:1-34

Am I always wanting to get something in return for my faith? Do I base decisions on what's best for the moment or what's best over the long haul? Am I spending enough time on the "food that endures to eternal life"?

Do I believe that I literally need Christ? Do I believe I need him every day, or just once in a while? What did Jesus mean when he said, "I am the bread of life"? Can I honestly say that Christ is the "bread" of my life?

JOHN
6:35-40

▼

Some believe that Jesus was simply a good man who said some nice things. But to say that Jesus was God—that Jesus came from heaven and that to believe in him is the only way to spiritual life—that's radical. Do I feel like Jesus really has given me life?

JOHN
6:41-51

▼

This sounds weird. What does Jesus mean when he says that we eat his flesh and drink his blood? When I take communion, do I sense the presence of Jesus differently than I do at other times? Does communion mean more or less to me each time I take it?

JOHN
6:52-59

JOHN
6:60-71

Jesus said that temporal things, external things, things of the flesh—that these things do not matter. Yet all around me they do matter. Do I really believe that the words of God are life-giving? Do I feel that God chose me as he chose the disciples? Do I really feel that without Jesus I would have nothing, or—like Peter felt—that I'd have nowhere to go?

▼

JOHN
7:1-19

Am I encouraged by this passage's reminder that I don't need seminary or graduate studies in order to understand the Bible? The crowds were amazed at Jesus' understanding—yet I have the same Holy Spirit to help me understand. Do I believe that my understanding of the Bible and God can be just as accurate and insightful as a scholar's?

▼

JOHN
7:20-31

Why did people want to kill Jesus? What did he do that made them so angry? He only did good things, helpful things. Does it help me understand that when I follow Christ, people around me may feel threatened and angry—even though I do good things? Jesus told his listeners to quit judging by appearances. Do I often judge people by how they look or how they talk without really knowing them?

▼

JOHN
7:32-52

Why do people believe in Jesus? Why do they not believe? Is belief a response to evidence, or is it a decision I make in spite of evidence? How can I convince my friends who don't believe in God to believe in him? The Pharisees were angry because even the guards were impressed with Jesus' words. Should I encourage my friends to read the words of Christ?

▼

Do I tolerate my own sins, yet condemn others for theirs? Jesus showed mercy, love, compassion, and strength. Do I try to develop those qualities in my life? What about mercy? Do I show mercy to those around me? Jesus forgave the woman but told her to sin no more. Do I realize that being forgiven of my sins does not mean that my sins don't matter? Do I ask God for forgiveness and the strength to sin no more?

JOHN 7:53-8:11

Jesus said that he "knew where he came from and where he was going." Do I have that same assurance and confidence in my life? Do I know where I came from and where I am going? Do I believe that God is reliable? Jesus said that he always did what pleased his Father. Do I do all I can to please him? What can I do to increase my desire to please him?

JOHN 8:12-30

"The truth will set you free"—what does that mean? Do I feel free? Does my faith make me feel free from sin? Free from the bondage of others' expectations? Free from dependence on drugs or alcohol or popularity? Jesus said to the unbelieving Pharisees, "He who belongs to God hears what God says. The reason you do not hear is that you do not belong to God." Does this mean that I understand God in ways that some of my friends don't yet? If so, what do I do? How can I help my friends know God as I know him?

JOHN 8:31-59

Do I believe that if I sin God will punish me by giving me cancer or causing an accident? Do I understand that God can be glorified even in a tragedy?

JOHN 9:1-5

JOHN 9:6-23

Here again are people who do not stand up for what they know is true because of fear (vv. 20-23). Have I ever refused to defend someone who was being made fun of because I was afraid of others?

▼

JOHN 9:24-41

When Jesus healed a blind man, giving him sight, the Pharisees were furious. They were so obsessed with their hatred of Jesus, they could see nothing else. Have I ever been obsessed with a girlfriend, boyfriend, new car, or job to the point that I didn't care what my parents or anyone else thought about me? How do I give up an obsession? How do I learn to listen to Jesus when I really don't want to give up an obsession?

▼

JOHN 10:1-21

Do I recognize the voice of Jesus? How do I know when Jesus tells me no? Who are the wolves in my life? How will Jesus protect me from them?

JOHN 10:22-42

When Jesus was again confronted by hostile unbelief, he tried to reason with them and respond to their questions—but still they refused to believe. Have I ever been confronted by hostile unbelief? What does this passage tell me to do when I am? Am I strong enough to firmly express my beliefs only to be met with an unwillingness to believe?

▼

JOHN 11:1-16

Jesus decided to risk returning to a hostile Judea for the sake of a friend. What am I willing to risk for my friends? Do I care enough about my friends' spiritual welfare to spend time praying for them, helping them, talking with them about my faith in Christ?

▼

Do I believe that Jesus will raise me? That although I die a bodily death, I will be raised anew by Christ? How does this belief affect my everyday life?

JOHN 11:17-27

▼

Do I remember that Jesus is capable of weeping, of showing genuine emotion? What does that say about how God cares for me? Do I appreciate his care and love for me?

JOHN 11:28-37

▼

Jesus actually raised someone from the dead. Do I really believe he did that? Could he still raise someone from the dead? Why doesn't he? Do I really believe Jesus has supernatural power that can be used today—right now—in my life?

JOHN 11:38-44

▼

The real issue with Jesus was power. The religious leaders were afraid that they would lose followers to Jesus, which would result in them losing their recognition by the Roman government and, consequently, their power over the people.

Isn't that the real issue in my own life—power? Am I willing to become powerless for the sake of Christ? Am I willing to give up the trappings of power and instead seek the real power that comes from knowing Christ? Jesus had no money, no home, no plan, no army—yet the powerful could do nothing against Jesus until he decided they could. That's power. Jesus said, "No man takes my life." He gave his life away. Do I have the power of Christ in my life so that I am no longer afraid of anyone or anything?

JOHN 11:45-57

▼

Have I ever been so caught up in my love for Jesus that I wanted to express that love extravagantly? Jesus rebuked Judas' supposed concern for the waste of money because Jesus

JOHN 12:1-8

knew he was a thief. What was Jesus saying?
Did he not care for the poor, or was he pointing
out that it is not contradictory to both care for
the poor and worship Jesus? Is it possible to do
both? Do I care enough about the needs of the
poor that it affects my pocketbook, or am I
concerned only in an intellectual way? Do I
worship Jesus with my possessions and my
tears, too?

▼

**JOHN
12:9-19**

Jesus finally won the acclaim of the crowd, but
it lasted not even a week. Has Jesus taught me
never to trust the whims of the crowd? Why is
the acclaim of a crowd such heady wine? Did
the crowd really come to honor Jesus because
of who he was, or did they want just more
tricks? Do I love Christ, or do I love what he
does for me? Do I praise, honor, and obey God
only when things go as I want them to? Would
I have stayed with Christ on Good Friday as
well as on Palm Sunday?

When the Greeks came to see Jesus, Jesus recognized it as a sign that his mission had spread to include the non-Jews (Gentiles) as well as the Jews. It was a sign that his time for dying on the cross was close at hand. As a seed must die before it can sprout, so Jesus had to first die.

JOHN
12:20-
26

Am I open to the signs God sends me? Have I ever seen a clear sign from God in my life? Do I realize that God sometimes sends me a sign telling me that a particular work I am doing, or a particular friendship must end? Am I willing to be governed by what God thinks is best instead of what I think is best? Do I realize that if my Christian life means anything at all, I must sometimes chose to do what I actually don't want to do—simply because God needs it done? Am I willing to trust God's wants more than my wants?

▼

Do I realize that Jesus was afraid of his approaching death and wanted to somehow avoid it? Do I realize therefore that Jesus will understand me when I feel weak and afraid of hardships? Am I willing to obey Christ even when I don't like the idea?

JOHN
12:27-
36

▼

God gives me a free will that I can use to blind myself to God's truth. How have I become blind to God? What are my blind spots? Girlfriend or boyfriend? Drinking? Drugs? Money? Job? Parents? Do I refuse God a free hand in certain areas in my life? Am I willing to open my whole life to the truth of God?

JOHN
12:37-
43

▼

Jesus said he came "not to judge the world, but to save it." Do I really believe in a God that is more interested in saving people than zapping them? Do I try and communicate to my friends and family the saving part of God? If we look at Jesus to see what God is like, what is God

JOHN
12:44-
50

like? That is, what does my knowledge of Jesus and his life on earth tell me about who God is?

▼

JOHN 13:1-11

Even though Peter and the other disciples protested vigorously against Jesus washing their feet, assuming that foot-washing was an inappropriate way for Jesus to serve them, they needed to learn how to receive. Do I allow Jesus to minister to me, to serve me? How? Do I recognize needs in me that Jesus alone can fill?

▼

JOHN 13:12-20

Do I realize that I am called to serve others in difficult, perhaps humbling ways just as Jesus served the apostles by washing their feet? Am I willing to serve others even when my efforts are rejected or unappreciated? Do I realize that when I refuse to serve others, I am actually refusing to serve Christ himself?

▼

JOHN 13:21-30

Do I realize that when I know what I'm about to do is seriously wrong, yet I push ahead and do it anyway—do I realize that I am betraying Jesus just as Judas did?

▼

JOHN 13:31-38

To demonstrate love is apparently how unbelievers will know I am a disciple of Christ. Do unbelievers around me know that I am in fact a disciple? How do I show love to my fellow Christians?

▼

JOHN 14:1-14

Am I aware that Jesus is working for me and with me even while he is with the Father in heaven? Do I really believe Jesus when he says that I not only can do many of the things that he did, but that I can do even greater things than he did if I follow his will and rely on his power?

Who has more influence on me—the Holy Spirit or the "ruler of this world"? Do I feel like an orphan, or do I feel the actual presence of the Holy Spirit in my life? Jesus said that one of the ways I show my love for him is to obey him. On the basis of my obedience to God, do people know I love him? Do I have the peace of God in my life, or do I feel anxious and stressed all the time? How can I become more a person of peace?

JOHN 14:15-31

▼

Jesus is the vine and I am one of the branches, he said. What does that mean? How can I bear fruit? What is this fruit? Am I bearing fruit now in my life?

JOHN 15:1-17

▼

Am I willing to be persecuted like Jesus was? Do I realize that the world hated Jesus without reason, and that I will likewise be hated and persecuted, not for doing bad, but for doing good? Will I despair and give up and become bitter when that happens—or will I rejoice because I am able to suffer with Christ and for Christ?

JOHN 15:18-16:4

▼

Do I realize that the Holy Spirit condemns many of the messages and values of the world as sinful? Am I aware that the prince of this world (Satan) has already been condemned and judged? Do I realize that Christ has given me the Holy Spirit to help me understand the Bible, to lead me closer to God, and to convict me of sin in my life? Do I realize that I am not alone—that God's Holy Spirit is my constant companion?

JOHN 16:5-16

▼

Do I realize how important it is to be patient? Do I ask God for patience? Do I know how to wait on God? Do I realize how important it is to endure? Am I willing to endure pain and

JOHN 16:17-24

suffering now so that later I will have joy? Am I willing, in other words, to put up with the limitations and frustrations and suffering that this world hands out to me, knowing there's another world coming where there will be no more pain or suffering?

▼

JOHN 16:25-33

The apostles thought they understood everything Jesus said, that they were prepared for anything. They were wrong, of course. Yet do I think that I know exactly what God says to me, do I feel prepared for any eventuality —when in fact I don't have the least inkling of what God is saying and I am utterly unprepared? Am I willing to ask God to strengthen my faith—even if the strengthening means that things have to get tougher for me?

▼

JOHN 17:1-26

Do I realize that Jesus is just as concerned about me and as willing to help me as he was about his apostles when he knew he had to leave them? Do I trust him to take care of me, or do I panic and fall back on my own strength and abilities?

▼

JOHN 18:1-11

How would I have reacted if I had been Jesus when the soldiers came to arrest him? How would I have reacted if I had been Peter or another of the apostles? How do I react now when my faith is threatened or when I am threatened? What can I learn from Jesus' response?

▼

JOHN 18:12-27

Caiaphas committed an insidious sin: he planted a seed in the minds of those who wanted Jesus dead. So they decided to kill Jesus because of this comment of Caiaphas. Have I ever been guilty of provoking others to sin by merely providing the suggestion? Have I ever been guilty of encouraging someone's anger or of supporting their intention to harm? Am I aware of how powerful an idea can be? Am I careful with my words and suggestions? Do I realize that Caiaphas was just as guilty of Jesus' death as if he had personally hammered the nails in Jesus' hands?

▼

Pilate was impressed by the wisdom and goodness of Jesus—but not impressed enough to save him from dying. Am I impressed with Jesus when it doesn't cost me anything, but deaf to him when it would cost me to follow him? How many times have I known something was wrong, only to go ahead and do it anyway? How can I become stronger in my faith so I don't yield to the pressure from others?

JOHN 18:28-38a

▼

The crowd refused to let Pilate off the hook. They demanded Jesus' death—and accepted nothing less.

JOHN 18:38b-19:16

Am I aware that evil doesn't compromise? Am I aware that evil always wants its way, no matter who it hurts or what it damages? Do I take evil seriously? Do I understand how dangerous it is for me to play with evil? Do I understand now why Paul said to flee from evil?

▼

JOHN 19:17-27

Is it hard for me to believe that Pilate was impressed enough with Jesus that he would not alter the notice posted on the cross—yet still let him die? Was Pilate much different from me, a believing Christian and impressed with Jesus—at the same time that I exclude him from crucial decisions of my life? Even in his dying moments, Jesus thought of the welfare of his mother and of his best friend, John. When I'm in the middle of hardship, do I think only of myself, or do I think of others around me who I love?

▼

JOHN 19:28-37

Do I realize that Jesus fulfilled many Old Testament passages by his death on the cross? Do I realize how many times the Old Testament speaks of a lamb being slain for the sins of the world? Have I considered that Jesus fulfilled the five Old Testament requirements for the sacrificial lamb: he was a male; he was a first-born child; he was unblemished (by sin); he suffered no broken bones; and all his blood was drained from his body (which happened to Jesus when the blood and water flowed from his side from the guard's spear wound)?

Do I understand that Jesus was the total fulfillment of Old Testament prophecy? He was the Messiah. He was the Lamb. Have I thanked God for sending his Son to be slain, sacrificed for me and my sin?

▼

Am I like Joseph and Nicodemus—a secret follower of Christ? How can I keep from being a secret follower of Christ? How can I let people know that I am a follower without being pushy or obnoxious about it?

JOHN 19:38-42

▼

John outran Peter to the tomb, but then waited until Peter stepped into the tomb before he entered himself. Do I have that kind of respect for authority? Do I respect older people and people in positions of authority? Do I respect my parents? My teachers? My church leaders? If I had been John or Peter, would I have believed—or would I have been like Thomas, who demanded to see the body before he would believe?

JOHN 20:1-10

▼

Mary Magdalene, formerly a notorious sinner, was so devoted to Jesus she couldn't stop crying. Have I ever allowed my emotions to dwell solely on Jesus and what he did for me? Have I ever cried over my Savior? Once Mary recognized Jesus, she wanted to hold on to him—but Jesus told her, no, rather go tell the others. Have I ever wanted to hold onto Jesus—to stay at a camp or church because I didn't want to go back into the real world of difficulties and pain? Do I prefer to spend time with Jesus rather than do the work of Jesus? How do I strike a balance between being with Jesus and actively serving him?

JOHN 20:11-18

▼

Jesus brought peace to the apostles, forgiving them for running away and accepting them as his friends. He then gave them power to bring peace and forgiveness to others. Though it is ultimately God who forgives, have I ever understood that I can also bring peace and forgiveness to others? Do I realize that people sometimes need another person to talk to? That they need to hear Christ's words of forgiveness

JOHN 20:19-23

and love from another's lips? Do I bring peace like this to my friends?

▼

JOHN 20:24-31

Do I demand signs that I can see or feel in order to believe that God is present? Do I understand that, although God honors our need to see and feel, he challenges us to believe without them? Yes, Jesus gave Thomas signs and he gives me signs. Yet will I accept the challenge of believing without visible evidence?

▼

JOHN 21:1-14

Through the miracle of the fishes, John and the other disciples recognized Jesus. Do I believe that Jesus does many things in my life that show his presence? Do I recognize the Lord through his providential actions in me? Do I anticipate daily the presence of the resurrected Christ in my life?

▼

JOHN 21:15-23

Because Peter denied Jesus three times, Jesus asked Peter to affirm him three times and to state that he loved him. When I blow it, when I sin, do I take time to assure Christ how much I love him? Do I carefully analyze my willingness to serve and follow Christ even though I've sinned? Do I tell God often how much I love him? Can I tell him right now?

▼

JOHN 21:24-25

John says that not all of Jesus' wondrous works, not all of his words were recorded. Could it be that even greater things than Jesus did can be done by his followers if they call upon his power? Could it be that I am capable of doing even greater things than the disciples?

Could it be up to me to keep the story going?